MONETS COOKERY NOTEBOOKS

Claude Monet c. 1880.

In memory of Marguerite.
These lines are affectionately dedicated
to Kaki de Cossé-Brissac
for obvious reasons.

Published by Ebury Press
an imprint of Century Hutchinson Ltd.
Brookmount House,
62–65 Chandos Place, Covent Garden,
London WC2N 4NW

French edition, *Les Carnets de Cuisine de Monet*, first published in 1989 by
Société Nouvelle des Editions du Chêne.

© 1989 Sté Nlle des Editions du Chêne

Translation © 1989 Century Hutchinson Ltd. and Simon & Schuster Inc.

British Library Cataloguing in Publication Data
Joyes, Claire
   Monet's Cookery Notebooks
   1. Food : French dishes - Recipes
   1. Title
   641.5944

ISBN 0 85223 825 8

Series editor: Marie-France Boyer
Art directors: François Huertas assisted by Philippe Pierrelée
English language edition edited by Alison Wormleighton

Typeset in Great Britain by Saxon Printing Ltd., Derby
Colour separation by Actual of Bienne, Switzerland
Printed in Italy by Canale of Turin

MONET'S COOKERY NOTEBOOKS

by
Claire Joyes

consultant
Jean-Marie Toulgouat

photography by
Jean-Bernard Naudin

foreword by
Joël Robuchon

English translation by
Pholiota Translations, London
(Josephine Bacon)

EBURY PRESS
LONDON

ACKNOWLEDGEMENTS

The photographic record in this book could not have been completed without the help of many people. I would especially like to express my gratitude to all those who helped me so much, entrusting many items to me so that I could accurately recreate the atmosphere of Monet's home. These include the Cristalleries de St. Louis, Haviland & Parlon, Gérard Danton, Alain Fassier, Christian Benais, Jean-Pierre de Castro, Constance Maupin, Madeleine Gely, Hubert Brugière, Artémise & Cunégonde, Jean-Claude Romain, Pierre G. Bernard, Fanette, La Tuile à Loup, Au Bon Usage, Au Puceron Chineur, Eric Dubois, Madame Est Servie, Galerie Paramythiotis, Nathalie Mabille de Villers in Arthies, Fauchon, Cassegrain, Ercuis, and La Créperie at Villers-en-Arthies. My special thanks go to Madame Nathalie Révillon, manageress of Maxim's Traiteur, who prepared all the dishes for photography with a genuine concern for their authenticity and with so much enthusiasm.

Nanou Billaut

I would like to take this opportunity of thanking Monsieur Gérard Van der Kemp of the Institute, Curator of the Claude Monet Museum, Madame Gérard Van der Kemp, who was unstinting in her enthusiasm for this project, and Madame Claudette Lindsey for her efficient and generous assistance, as well as Madame Nathalie Mabille, and Mademoiselle Catherine Gourdain.

Claire Joyes

CONTENTS

FOREWORD 9

THE TASTE OF AN ERA 13

A Turn of the Century Table 15
*The development of
Monet's cuisine*

The Rotunda Drawing Room 23
*The Hoschedés and
Château de Rottenbourg*

LIFE AT GIVERNY 31

Pride of Place 33
*Creating a home and
a retreat from the world*

Florimond's Kitchen-Garden 41
*Imposing order upon nature,
for the benefit of the table*

LIFE WITH MONET AND ALICE 51

The Family Table 53
Domestic life and the daily routine

Picnics and Celebration Lunches 65
Rituals to celebrate the rhythm of the seasons

Birds of Passage 97
Family excursions and special visitors

THE RECIPES 109

Soups 111 · Eggs 115 · Sauces 118

Appetisers and Side Dishes 123 · Poultry 131

Meat 137 · Game 147 · Fish 153 · Desserts 165

Teas 179 · Jams 182 · Preserves 183

INDEX

General 185 · Recipes 187

FOREWORD

Having abandoned my native Poitou, I became a Parisian by adoption, to better practise the art I so loved. In 1980, while I was working as the *chef de cuisine* at the Hotel Nikko, I visited Claude Monet's house in Giverny; I remember the occasion very vividly.

The garden flowers blended into a harmonious color scheme and the decor and design of the painter's beautiful home were so innovative that I was greatly moved by them.

Inside the house, the large, chrome-yellow dining room left me with the impression of a lavishly run household. I very much liked the huge, simply decorated, blue-tiled kitchen with its array of equipment and utensils, which for me evoked the delicious food that had been so lovingly prepared here. Perhaps this is where I unconsciously conceived the idea of the future ideal restaurant.

That day, a thought suddenly came to me. Wouldn't it be wonderful to one day discover this family's culinary secrets, and to have the immense pleasure of

eventually recreating them? Now that Claude Monet's cookery notebooks have been revealed and published, thanks to Claire Joyes and Jean-Marie Toulgouat, this has actually become possible.

I very much enjoyed adapting the recipes, and have carefully checked them to make sure that you will have no difficulty in making these dishes.

In order to get to know the artist better and discover his personality through his lavish cuisine, I read a great deal, and this enabled me to get to know this giant among men, a great man who had been able to overcome all the vicissitudes of life.

His friends and biographers relate that he had a hearty appetite, but that he was discerning and even extremely fussy about food. For his many guests — including Clemenceau, Renoir, and Pissarro — and for his family, he carved game, roasts, and poultry himself at the table. He preferred foie gras from Alsace and truffles from Périgord. He adored fish, especially the pike from his own pond. He had a kitchen-garden which was scrupulously maintained, and in which he grew herbs,

potherbs, vegetables from the Midi, and field mushrooms which were carefully picked at dawn.

I was delighted by the discovery of the recipes, because they are a real palette of tastes, yet full of common sense, for use in the service of a simple, bourgeois and tasty cuisine. Some of them are extremely simple, others more difficult, requiring a certain amount of professionalism, which was quite an achievement for the period. It should not be forgotten that none of the equipment was available which we find so indispensable today. Giverny did not even possess an ice-box!

For your inventiveness, for your great generosity, for all these beautiful and great recipes, for these precious journals, the evidence of the great cooking of the past, for this wonderful lifestyle,

Thank you, Claude Monet.

JOËL ROBUCHON
Chef de Cuisine
Restaurant Jamin, Paris

THE TASTE OF AN ERA

Autumn 1900.
Marthe's marriage
to Theodore Butler
brought family and
friends together for
a celebratory
luncheon.

A Turn of the Century Table

'*February 4, 1884.*
Tasted a banana for the first time in my life, I
won't do it again until purgatory.'

JULES RENARD, *DIARY*

*I*f a house has character, the fact is obvious immediately. Claude Monet's house at Giverny certainly did, down to the smallest details of its kitchen. With its essentially bourgeois character, this house, and its large walled garden, became for Monet a perfect haven. It was his own separate world, from which he drew continual inspiration for over 40 years.

Monet always retained the predilection for over-indulgence that was characteristic of the French middle class at this period, and Giverny provided a place where he could enjoy his taste for the good life to the full. This instinctive, physical enjoyment of life was also the basis for Monet's painting. For him, painting was never applied theory – it was a practical reality. Heedless of references to the past, he lived for the present; he was very much a man of his times.

Monet's cookery notebooks do include a few faint traces of unconscious nostalgia, a flavour of the Restoration or the Second Empire, which, of course, was recent history in those days. Yet the notebooks mostly contain innovations of the Third Republic, combined with a few old

Opposite: At Giverny, the place settings were prepared in the kitchen before the table was laid.

Right: Claude Monet, *Luncheon on the Grass* (left-hand fragment), 1865-1866. Paris, Musée d'Orsay.

favourites, and seasoned with those exotic touches people have craved since our ships conquered the spice route on the high seas.

Eating well was something to which Monet had always been accustomed. There is little information available about the meals that were eaten in the family home in Le Havre, where he spent most of his childhood. By all accounts, his boyhood was spent in bourgeois comfort. His father was in business as a supplier to the navy, and his mother is supposed to have been an excellent hostess and to have entertained her guests with after-dinner songs, as she had a very pretty voice. Monet was less than 20 years old when she disappeared, and all the memories of the rituals of Le Havre faded into oblivion with her.

In 1860, Monet drew an unlucky number in the lottery for selective military service and served with the Chasseurs d'Afrique regiment in Algeria. The landscape and light did not prove too harsh for his liking, and, in fact, he claimed that Algeria inspired the earliest of his visual impressions. Yet he never discussed the food he ate there. It is impossible to believe that he never tasted and enjoyed that aromatic cuisine, simmered in earthenware pots on rudimentary little hearths, those delicious dishes so skilfully cooked over charcoal.

Monet was only 20 when he went to North Africa, but he had already held

exhibitions of his works and had established friendships with Boudin, Pissarro, Cézanne, Courbet and a number of other young men who were destined to become leading figures in the arts in the coming years.

After his return from Algeria in 1862, Monet began to work with Boudin, Jongkind, Renoir, Bazille and Sisley. His rebellion against the art establishment was becoming apparent, and his family responded to his seeming intransigence by cutting off his allowance. Poverty began to bite, as he had as yet very little income from his work. But though accustomed to a degree of comfort, and passionate about his food, Monet was prepared to make any sacrifice, undergo any discomfort for the sake of his art.

It was at about this time, in the mid 1860s, that Monet painted Camille Doncieux. They began living together, had a child, Jean, and married in 1870. With the outbreak of the Franco-Prussian War, Monet went to England, where he was influenced by the paintings of Turner and Constable, and where he developed a taste for a number of English dishes. He returned to France the following year, via the Netherlands, discovering more dishes that were to remain firm favourites.

In 1871, Monet, Camille and Jean settled in Argenteuil, a village on the Seine near Paris, famous for its boating. They remained there for six years. This marked a turning point in Monet's life, the restless, poverty-stricken bohemian existence of the previous decade being replaced by stability and relative comfort. Though always short of cash and continually in debt, Monet had actually begun to earn a reasonable living from his paintings. He acquired a boat, which he used as a studio for painting trips on the river, pursuing his fascination with water. It was at the charming, vine-covered cottage in Argenteuil that Monet created his first garden, reflecting his lifelong

Below: The annual Côte de Gaillon race was an occasion for this family of car- and picnic-lovers to get together.

delight in flowers. Here, too, no doubt, he was able to indulge his other great passion, food.

1874 was another landmark in Monet's life, when Monet and his friends, including Renoir, Sisley, Pissarro, Degas and Berthe Morisot, staged their first group exhibition. The uniformly hostile reaction of the press, who christened the group 'Impressionists', was a clear indication of the resistance the new movement would encounter over the coming years.

From 1878 to 1881, Monet rented a house at Vétheuil, further down the Seine, about 40 miles from Paris. Camille was by this time very ill. Monet, Camille, Jean and their second son, Michel, shared the house with Alice Hoschedé and her six children; Alice and her husband, former patrons of Monet, had recently been financially ruined and had separated. Following the death of Camille in 1879, the family lived as one, and Alice Hoschedé became Monet's second wife in 1892, after her estranged husband's death.

In his continuous struggle to impose his painting style, Monet was inhibited by the ever-present financial worries and the frustrating absence of a space large enough for him to work in comfortably. It was only at

Above:
Veuve Clicquot champagne was often drunk at Giverny.

Opposite: In summer, the garden was a riot of colour.

Giverny, which he discovered in 1883, that Monet was able to establish the lifestyle that really suited him. It was here that his ideas about food took shape, and Alice Hoschedé was to be their principal interpreter. Between them, Monet and Alice created their own art of living, something that today would be called style.

Their sole culinary ambition was to serve beautifully prepared dishes using whatever the kitchen-garden or the farmyard could supply. This was their food, home-made but often making use of recipes invented by the great restaurants they patronised, or even dishes created by their friends, who included writers, art collectors, painters and actors.

Many of the dishes can, of course, be

found in other cookbooks, but the recipe for the Monets' *bouillabaisse* came from Paul Cézanne and the recipe for their bread rolls from Jean Millet. Their *tarte Tatin* was a souvenir of their visits to the Tatin sisters themselves, to sample this famous dish. Origins such as these add zest to the dishes for us today, just as they undoubtedly did for the Monets a century ago.

Monet and Alice had decided to live out of town but not actually in the provinces. The house at Giverny was not one of those lonely country houses where one can relax far from the exhausting frenzy of the big city. Their life was a charming amalgam of a deliberately simple, rustic lifestyle with all its attendant pursuits, combined with the tolerant, but totally independent attitude to life which is typical of the inhabitants of a vast metropolis. It was a rural idyll in which urban values had been transposed to the countryside.

In the magnificent era of fin-de-siècle France, eating habits were still somewhat in a state of confusion; the art of good living only emerged with difficulty after much trial and error. Haute cuisine was still in its infancy, and even the compilation of menus was of recent invention.

During this period, in which France's constitution changed more frequently than her eating habits, quantity reigned supreme. A few eccentrics – whom some complimented with the epithet 'æsthete', but who were, in fact, the precursors of our

modern dieticians – urged greater sobriety and discernment, but in vain.

It is remarkable how much was accomplished in matters of custom and taste in a relatively short time. This applies not only to eating habits but also to the ingredients. The dishes Monet so enjoyed, such as *soles à la normande*, were born at virtually the same time as he was.

Taste is a complex subject. Not only is it highly personal but it also must always be considered in context. For example, in 1888, the desserts which Monet and everyone else liked and which seem to us today to be rather heavy, such as the *galette de plomb* (a flat cake made with cream), featured in the menu served to President Carnot in the train which took him to the Dauphiné region. In an era that was rather slow-moving, when it took eight hours to travel by train to a town that today is only two hours away, this was a perfectly suitable menu. The same applies to the secret recipes of the Maison Dorée, the Café Anglais or Chez Hardy, which took their time to percolate down to the tables of the middle classes or along the length of the Seine Valley. In any case, local shops needed to be stocked, and the markets provisioned with the right ingredients.

Even though this style of cooking may

be complicated, requiring the mistress of the house to be a master of organisation, what a reward it is to be served food that is fresh and in season!

From the vantage point of our modern age – in which Japanese dine in Paris with Venetians from London or Americans from Brussels – looking back on these more parochial times inevitably creates a certain nostalgia. In those days, green peas were not sent great distances if it could be helped because it was believed that they would lose their sweetness. There is a lot of truth in this. We have come a long way from that lost luxury of freshness. Nevertheless, against all odds, a few diehards have continued to worship at the almost abandoned shrine of the 'home-made'.

Below: Monet in his garden. Although he liked cottage gardens, Monet did not entirely escape from the contemporary taste for formal landscaping.

The Rotunda Drawing Room

'*And that bleached velum gilded by Clovis Eve*
Evokes who knows what faded charm
The soul of their fragrance and the shadow their dream.'

HEREDIA

Some houses rule us more than we rule them. The shape of a room in the great Château de Rottenbourg was to throw everyone's life into confusion, for it was the rotunda drawing-room here that brought Monet and Alice together.

Paris at the time was in the grip of a frenzy. Albert Wolf wrote in *Le Figaro* that five or six rebels, including a woman – who was none other than Berthe Morisot – had become involved in an exhibition organised by the art dealer Paul Durand-Ruel. The lurid details included the account of a man who had to be arrested at the exit because he was biting the passers-by. One hostile critic, seizing upon the unassuming title of Monet's painting, *Impression: Sunrise*, had tried to ridicule the group by christening them 'Impressionists'. In fact, the label was so apt that it was quickly adopted by the artists themselves.

Every hostess who prided herself on being avant-garde vied for the company of these rebels. Ernest Hoschedé, an art-collector and patron of the arts to his very soul, was immune to this kind of flamboyance. But although he knew that Impressionist painting did not necessarily

Opposite: The famous yellow water-lilies at the height of summer.

Pages 24-27: The garden in summer. Though near Paris, it was like being at the world's end.

cause the beholder to fly into a rage, he had not yet discovered that painting in general can lead to one's downfall.

Alice, his wife, was an extremely well-heeled young lady. Her family, the Raingos, sold art bronzes and expensive clocks to the royal courts of Europe, including the Tuileries Palace. They also reproduced Jacob Petit models and were in effect, what we would call today, the 'pacesetters' in Belgian society in Paris. On her father's death, Alice had inherited the Château de Rottenbourg, located at Montgeron in Normandy, and Ernest had devoted much time to refurbishing it. When it came to redecorating the large rotunda drawing-room, he thought of Monet. On that fateful September day in 1876, Monet was anxiously awaited and his arrival caused a sensation. It was this arrival which Alice's daughter, Blanche, chose to recall in her all-too-brief memoirs.

Of course, no one detected the first crack which threatened the whole structure. Monet, who so loved the countryside, was penniless once again and had every reason to rejoice in the opportunity of exchanging his money worries for the

serenity of the extensive grounds in which to paint, and the carefree life at the château.

The garden at Montgeron was a confusion of styles, but displayed a certain gauche charm with its too sharply delineated flower-beds, its Medici urns, and the romantic style of its landscaping.

The Hoschedés were lavish hosts, and set a fast pace, driving their families mad with the confusion in which they left their finances.

Ernest spent a lot of time in Paris, as busy unearthing rare art treasures as he was attending to his business affairs. Alice and her children spent more time at Rottenbourg; she loved it there. A socialite, quite excitable, very pious and something of a mystic, Alice was an attentive hostess and very lively, but sensitive and easily tired. Today she might be described as a cyclical manic depressive. She loved the countryside but had great need for company; Rottenbourg, with its proximity to Paris, attracted many visitors.

Ernest was one of the first collectors of the new schools of painting. He paid high prices for the paintings because he was a generous man, as Monet knew only too well. Unfortunately, he had to part with a few of his treasures to ward off the abyss which was threatening to – and did eventually – engulf him.

At Montgeron, the Hoschedés lived a life which combined frivolity with intellectual pursuits and which could be considered avant-garde. Ernest, the ostentatious playboy, would bring his guests from the Gare de Lyon in Paris by private train. Ernest and Alice seemed to be living in a daydream. Life was a mad whirlwind; everything glittered, a little too much.

The frequent visitors who were traditionalists mingled happily with those who were avant-garde. The Impressionist paintings by Sisley, Manet or Monet did not displace the family portraits, of which the most recent were signed by J.J. Henner, Carolus Duran, Benjamin Constant or Baudry.

Carolus Duran was one of the traditionalist painters who frequented Montgeron. Carolus was amusing, he had no doubts about anything, especially not himself, and he was quite right because he was extremely talented. He frequented numerous salons of which he was often the official portraitist. In fact, he has left us one of the rare existing portraits of Monet. He was incredibly charming and fascinated everyone by his conversation, which was something of a monologue. He danced, rode horses, sang, played the piano like everyone else, but also played the organ and was an excellent pistol shot. He lived quite close by and often came over to pay a neighbourly call and enliven the evenings. He remained close friends with Monet.

On the avant-garde side, there was Georges Charpentier, the publisher, who founded *La Vie Moderne*, an excellent magazine condemned by its very quality to a short lifespan. Charpentier had the brilliant idea of organising one-man shows of paintings at the magazine's offices, an extremely daring move for the times. Renoir exhibited there, as did Monet.

It was difficult to work in the atmosphere of a perpetual fun-fair. Yet Ernest, ever the attentive host, had thought of everything, and a pavilion, originally built as an orangery, away from the house, served Monet as a studio. In wanting to immortalise Rottenbourg, Ernest might almost have had a premonition.

He left it to Monet to choose the subject matter that seemed best to express the spirit of the place. Monet decided to decorate the rotunda drawing room with panels depicting the white turkey-cocks who strutted through the park, the massed dahlias by the pool and the pool itself. He later added a hunting scene, showing figures in the undergrowth, including Ernest himself in the foreground.

Monet remained at Rottenbourg for a long time, and managed to produce a lot of work there, but it is not known if Camille ever came to join him. It was only when they returned to Paris that the Hoschedé and Monet families – parents and children – became really close friends. There is at least

one park engraved in the memories of the youngest members of the family.

While Monet was staying at Montgeron, Alice perceived the unmistakable signs of shaky finances. Ernest was spending less and less time there and seemed to be increasingly preoccupied. She was gradually left more alone with her children, the servants and the company of an artist who produced very brilliant work. This gave her plenty of time in which eventually to compare her overgrown child of a husband with this simple but reliable man.

The spectre of ruin hovered in the background. Nevertheless, Ernest, an enthusiastic supporter of the Impressionists to the bitter end, bought three new canvases from Monet in the following year, 1877. Then, in August of that year, he was declared bankrupt. The whole of that summer, until September, passed in inventory-takings, court-ordered auctions and other horrors. About 50 Impressionist paintings in his collection were sold, all at ridiculously low prices. The twelve canvases by Monet fetched an average of only 184 francs each.

After some terrible tribulations including a number of humiliating episodes, the ruined Hoschedés with their six children, Marthe, Blanche, Suzanne, Jacques, Germaine and Jean-Pierre, plus a housemaid, governess and cook, moved in with Camille and Claude Monet – who were themselves impoverished – at Vétheuil.

LIFE AT GIVERNY

Monet and Butler
sitting in the family
automobile waiting to
be driven to market,
an important weekly
ritual in the
household.

Pride of Place

*'From the debris of the palace
I built my cottage.'*

SULLY PRUD'HOMME

Above: This black-and-white photo shows how the house was shrouded in luxuriant vegetation.

Opposite: The entrance hall at Giverny.

Camille died at Vétheuil after a lengthy illness, and Alice and Ernest were separated. It will never be known whether it was courage or a wider vision that motivated Madame Hoschedé, who was so conventional, so religious, and who valued respectability so highly, to share her life with Monet and bring up his two sons, Jean and Michel.

They arrived at Giverny in late April and early May, 1883, with their eight children, the youngest of whom was less than five years old. The move had been expensive and was staggered over a period of about six days, punctuated with the financial disruptions which had surreptitiously entered their everyday lives. They had a vast horde of possessions, which were brought down the Seine in their four boats. However, their baggage included the best of weapons with which to confront the unknown – a magnificent appetite for life, supported by an almost unconscious ability to rapidly forget the past. On their way down, they had shed their cook, their governess, and even Alice, that generous housemaid who had insisted on remaining in their service without wages after Rottenbourg had been sold.

Alice Hoschedé had been used to a life of great affluence, and she had now committed herself to an impoverished artist. This showed much daring on her part, especially in view of the age in which she lived. She now exchanged Rottenbourg in favour of a simple, converted farmhouse.

In truth, Monet and Alice were unaware of their good fortune, because the real luxury of Giverny was the fact that they had no close neighbours and that they were the lucky owners of a walled garden. This type of garden not only makes the best use of microclimates, it is also an excellent way of ensuring privacy.

Monet could not have found a better retreat than this elongated house, called the Maison du Pressoir (House of the Cider Press), which was so quickly transformed, and rendered slightly more bourgeois with fairly successful results. It had a good north-south aspect, and overlooked a garden sloping gently down to wide meadows – which at that time of year were a sea of flowers and plants. Next to the meadows lay a field of wild irises, overshadowed by ancient pollarded willows. The fruit-trees which covered the hills were in blossom; a delightful little train puffed along between the river and the narrow, twisting road at the bottom of the garden, known as the Chemin du Roy (the King's Way); and the washing-stones down by the water were a meeting-place where the village women could exchange gossip.

So close to Paris, yet one was at the world's end!

Monet and Alice couldn't afford an architect to work on the house, so they restricted themselves to straightforward alterations. Both were aware of the benefits of planting new vines and rambling roses, which will hide and beautify the ugliest of walls. There were a lot of outhouses: basements, cellars, lean-tos, all of them absolutely essential for the running of the household.

Although the countryside was so lovely, the same could not be said of the garden Monet had inherited, with its conifers and its rigidly geometrical layout. It lay in the midst of the orchard of plum-trees which looked so promising that year. This must have been the subject of some interesting conversations with Monet's friends, the artist Caillebotte and the playwright Mirbeau.

There was still enough room for plants with which to decorate the house and supply the table. Monet, helped by his children, immediately began sowing aromatics and flower seeds, so as to have something to pick for painting when the weather was bad. They planted annual chrysanthemums, poppies and large sunflowers. For the table, there was still time from July to September to grow romaine lettuce, spinach, peas, and radishes. Time was short, and they had so much to do, making themselves comfortable and starting to paint.

They did not yet know that, by the time the flowers had taken up all the available space, they would be able to acquire another garden as big as the first, the large garden attached to the Maison Bleue (the Blue House) in the village, which would become their kitchen-garden.

As for their beloved boats, they had set

their sights on a mooring at the Ile aux Orties (Nettle Island), an island in the Seine, where the rowing-boat, the two mahogany skiffs and the studio-boat were tied up. They were certain that this island would belong to them one day, and it features in many canvases painted at Giverny. Monet posed Suzanne, Alice's daughter, on it to paint *Lady with a Parasol*. Monet and Alice set to work at once making improvements, because there was something about the place which would otherwise make you die of boredom if you did not take action.

Yet how could these people who had recently been so impoverished suddenly start to rebuild Babylon? The answer is very simple. In addition to the Impressionists' admirers, who were more numerous than has been acknowledged, there was a person in Paris to whom they owed almost everything, although they never thought of it that way.

This was Paul Durand-Ruel – a man whose family had begun to doubt his sanity. Durand-Ruel was a businessman, as well as a patron of the arts, and he did some banking and financing on the side. Durand-Ruel, the 'Monsieur Durand' referred to by Renoir, Sisley, Pissarro, Monet and everyone else, was certainly not indifferent to making money, but he took the ultimate risk of acquiring canvases by all these artists. He advanced them the funds they needed for survival, although sometimes

Pages 36-37: The kitchen was painted in brilliant pale blue to match the tiles. The kitchen and the studio were the two sacrosanct rooms of the house.

the paintings he bought from them had not even left the studio. He thus acquired hundreds of paintings which were difficult to sell, since it is always hard to be ahead of one's time. Monet's creditors would present themselves at the gallery and Durand-Ruel would settle the cost of schooling for the children, settle the accounts of the artists' materials supplier and the framer, and even pay Monet's tailor. Monet always dressed well whatever his financial circumstances.

That is how the pinkish-ochre, rough-cast exterior came to be darkened, the grey shutters repainted in Neti green, similar in colour to Veronese green, and a long, wooden balcony built to run the length of the house. A new kitchen was added over the cellar and a suite of two rooms over the barn, which had been transformed into a studio. The kitchen and the studio, two sacrosanct spots, were the first to be subjected to major rebuilding.

Monet and Blanche decided on pale colours for the walls, pastel tones, except in the dining-room which was painted in pale and medium chrome yellow. The dining-room led into a blue room. Whether one opened the door of the kitchen, the small entrance-hall or the mauve drawing-room, there was an escalation, a progression of colour from cobalt blue, through madder to white. All these hues were created by Monet and were the subject of lengthy discussions with the village house-painter,

who took a while to recover from his astonishment! The staircases, narrow corridors, and the two dressing-rooms, as well as the bathroom with its huge, friendly copper water-heater, were painted in a more English colour scheme of white, offset here and there by a touch of blue or madder. The girls' rooms were more acid in tone.

Finally, there was the suite of rooms occupied by Alice and Monet. They overlooked a lovely little hill which served them as a natural barometer, bathed as it often was in a bluish, opalescent haze, the poetic counterpart of the barometer on the wall which Monet was never without. The walls were adorned with damask tablecloths sewn together.

Above: Blue-leaved water-lilies in the pond.

Opposite: The ancient ice-cream maker, which was essential equipment for making the banana ice-cream served on Christmas Day.

The kitchen, which was to be constantly modernised, has been handed down to us in the state which was the ultimate in rural comfort just prior to World War I. The walls and ceiling sparkled with a bright-blue gloss paint which matched the blue Rouen tiles. These tiles were to be found in all the local kitchens, just as it was the custom in this part of the country to tile the chimneypieces. Nothing could be a better complement to the array of copper pots and pans than those plain little Rouen tiles. The white porcelain hanging lamp would take over from the daylight which streamed in through the windows, unhindered by any curtains. That monolithic monument, the stove – the altar on which flavours depend – had pride of place.

Florimond's Kitchen-Garden

'*At present, lowly guardian of fruits and salads*
I defend this enclosure against marauders...'

JOSÉ MARIA DE HEREDIA

Above: Claude Monet, *Still Life with Melon*, 1876. Gulbenkian Museum.

Opposite: Peaches were grown in the kitchen-garden run by Florimond.

*I*t is the habits of a lifetime that determine whether a house will survive, prosper or decline. But half a century later, it is virtually impossible completely to unravel chains of events – to pinpoint exactly when particular habits crept in, or to analyse how those imperceptible changes occurred which give places their character and style.

Although Monet took an interest in everything, and was certainly not one to retire into an ivory tower, Alice and the two daughters who succeeded her, Marthe then Blanche, ran the house according to a host of immutable rituals. What is disconcerting is their Benedictine-like adherence to a strict timetable at Giverny (make no mistake, the true Benedictine of the place was Monet), even though the recreation each day was itself relatively carefree. The activities might fluctuate between, say, observing the rose-beetles who lived exclusively on a diet of rose-leaves in the garden, 'tinkering with bicycles' (as Alice described the boys' experiments with mechanical inventions), canoeing, photography, picnics, plus lessons in Latin and botany from the local parish priest, Abbé Toussaint.

The family's time was occupied in a private life that was very affectionate and loving, even demanding. There were live-in staff who were integrated into a clearly defined emotional background, which was both close and distant at the same time. Some individuals would control a particular domain. There was a succession of gardeners and cooks, and those chosen for the task had to know how to prepare the kind of food that Monet liked and landscape his garden the way he envisaged it.

Right: Claude Monet, *The Basket of Grapes*, Paris. Private collection.

Below left: Germaine and Sisi leaving for a picnic on the Ile aux Orties (Nettle Island).

Thus, Marguerite (whom the author knew well) presided over the kitchen, Félix over the garden and Sylvain over the wine-cellar, the studio and above all the cars. Paul was responsible for various missions of trust in the house and flower-garden, while Florimond ruled the kitchen-garden.

The farmyards were only a few steps away from the blue-painted kitchen. Some turkeys were raised here, goodness knows why, but they were not white like those at Rottenbourg. Turkey-rearing was soon abandoned, however, because they are not very dainty creatures, and no one in the household liked eating turkey. Nevertheless, it was amusing to have some farm animals around.

The upper farmyard, which was reserved for the ducks, had a pond in which they could dabble. Nearby, there was another pond for watering, and a nesting

tree, as well as clumps of shrubbery, because ducks like to keep their nests hidden away. This little enclosure was home to Nantes ducks and White Indian Runners, whose females were excellent layers, but might be outdone by the Khaki Campbells. There were also some exquisite little Mandarin ducks which had been bought for the sole pleasure of looking at them. Barbary and Rouen ducks were banned, however, since they were considered to be too fatty.

Monet was so fanatical about the poultry he was served at table that he took an inordinate amount of time choosing ducks and hens to be used for breeding stock. He haunted the breeders and bird-sellers, because he considered the local farmers to be too unselective in their breeding techniques.

In the hen yard, where three or four different breeds were being reared, the situation was quite complicated. Houdans, who were sought after for their laying capacity as well as their flesh, clucked away with beautiful white Gâtinaise hens and plump black Bresse hens, and there were also a few Cayenne hens which had been presented as gifts by friends. These were sometimes joined by the odd pheasant.

The job of running the farmyard is usually that of the gardener, but it was Blanche who throughout her life, whenever she could, fed the ducks and hens. Although Paul, Marguerite's husband, had

Above: In the summer, the nasturtiums invaded the avenue leading to the front door.

been promoted to valet and butler, he would remove the eggs, supervise the rearing and keep things tidy. He had to try to maintain order among the different breeds, stopping the Faverolles hens from dethroning the Houdan dynasties. He even had to keep a sort of register of births, marriages and deaths, because certain breeds require the careful selection of cockerels to keep their egg-laying performance high, which is very important in winter.

Fortunately, Monet detested domesticated rabbit and would only eat hare and wild rabbit, so there were no hutches. Nor were there dovecotes, because pigeons were bought from Duboc or Ledanois. There were so many different types of farm in the area that they did not lack suppliers.

Next to the second studio, which Monet had erected near the lime trees, there was an aviary. It was little more than a sickbay for unusual or wounded birds, and here all sorts of boarders were accommodated. They included the gulls sent from Belle-Ile by Monet for the 'little ones', that is, Michel and Jean-Pierre, who would thus have an excellent excuse for going fishing. After all, the gulls needed feeding.

*U*ndoubtedly, a powerful spirit of organisation breathed through this household, in which no good food was possible without a kitchen-garden. In this respect, the kitchen-garden was a work of art, one of the things of which Monet was justifiably most proud. In his mind, this vegetable garden was inseparable from the other things that to Monet were part of the good life – his flower-garden, the farm-yards, a well-aged wine bottled by Sylvain, a well-cut suit, Marguerite's excellent cooking and a good read in the studio-drawing room.

The two-and-a-half acre walled kitchen-garden, which stood at the opposite end of the village, in the rue du Chêne, was the exact counterpart of the flower-garden. Both had the same aspect, receiving the sun all day, and both were terraced in

Above: The house in summer with the garden in full bloom.

Opposite: Preparing pike with white butter sauce for Sunday lunch (recipe on page 157).

the same style. However, the slope of the kitchen-garden was steeper, and it was squarer, which made the arrangement of the sections easier and more attractive.

Everything that was banned from the flower-garden was strongly advocated here in the kitchen-garden. There was a strict geometrical plan and paths were laid out in straight lines, to enable the work to be carriedly out logically, rapidly and with minimum effort.

Doyenne de Comice and Beurré d'Hardempont pear-trees were espaliered along the sunny walls. Separated from them by a little path there were horizontally strung espaliers for 'the apple harvest' of the Reine des Reinettes russets required for the upside-down apple tart, *tarte Tatin*. Few trees are needed in a kitchen-garden. The only ones allowed in Monet's were the long- and short-stemmed Montmorency cherry trees, as well as greengage plum-trees and Petite yellow plum-trees. These fruits were used by Marguerite to make her famous brandied preserves and the compotes of cherries preserved in their own juice. A few quince-trees and some ornamentals had also been planted.

Along with the garden in the rue du Chêne, Monet had purchased the house attached to it, known as the Maison Bleue (the Blue House). Florimond was installed here. He frequently needed the help of one or two gardeners from the main garden because the fruit and vegetable harvest was so abundant, to say nothing of the meticulous irrigation which had to be performed with the aid of an ill-tempered pump that made the devil of a noise.

A variety of cultivated plants grew cheek by jowl, native plants being cultivated side-by-side with those from warmer climates. The space available was by no means too large considering the demanding nature and large appetites of the family.

Monet bought seeds and plants every-

where he went, bartering with other gardeners; he adored trying to grow the most delicate shoots as if to challenge the climate at Giverny. It was he who leafed through the catalogues and ordered from them.

He also insisted on the age-old custom that the garden be laid out with root vegetables, leaf vegetables, bulbs and seeds, grouped in their own sections. Perfect order was the rule, even down to the arrangement of the cold-frames, the pyramids of pots for planting out melons and the piles of cloches. There were trenches for Jerusalem artichokes, grown mainly as potherbs, and rows in which certain vegetables had to be grown, such as the red cabbage Monet had a passion for.

All this denoted an absolute and disciplined layout worthy of a town-planning map. There was no shortage of right-angles here! One could stroll along paths lined with climbing vegetables, along avenues of Milan cabbages, brussels sprouts or broccoli, beside rows of romaine lettuces, celery, pale chicory or Paresseux de Castillon spinach. One crossroads, which was marked by a rosemary bush, was bordered with thyme, chives and savory for the broad beans, and even Belleville garlic for the *sauce verte*. Sage and oregano, with their blue flowers, dotted the edge of the path. Tarragon, however, cannot be grown to order; wherever it wants to develop it should be left to itself.

The sheltered, terraced area was

Opposite: Monet and his daughters-in-law with the first American painters to visit Giverny.

Pages 48-49: Although the layout of the garden at Giverny was geometric, this was obscured by the colourful, lush borders.

reserved for plants from more southern climes. There were red, yellow and cherry tomatoes, Vert de Provence globe artichokes to be eaten raw when young, chillis, sweet peppers, Nice courgettes, all of them unknown in this region, as well as broad beans and French beans, rocamboles (a member of the onion family), and oriental garlic, and those little Egyptian pearl onions which taste so delicious when pickled in vinegar.

Florimond was an expert in growing crosnes, a vegetable Monet loved. He was also very proud to bring his early vegetables to the kitchen from mid-February.

Florimond knew Monet's rages if the vegetables were not picked at the right time, yet nothing was more difficult. Every day, Monet would select from the vegetables ordered the previous day, and on Sunday he would choose those for the stockpot, which was indispensable for the preparation of soups and stocks for the whole week.

The seed catalogues Monet so often studied were soon to become the relics of a vanishing era – a time when Paris grew almost everything it needed on its own doorstep, before those fields of cultivated blooms in the market-gardens and every kind of small farm were swamped under a rising tide of buildings and factories.

LIFE WITH MONET AND ALICE

Menu for the
wedding luncheon
of Germaine
Hoschedé and
Albert Salerou.

The Family Table

'I have built my home among humans
but no sound of a horse nor a carriage matters to me
— How is that possible?
— To a distant heart, everything is a retreat.'

TAO YUANMING

who had no particular vocation, organised the work of all the servants, and was hostess to relatives, Monet's friends and the art-dealers. Like all those who are familiar with the ways of the world, she knew how to modulate her attitude, her vocabulary and her menus to suit her guests. There were those who needed to be impressed a little and others where this would have been insensitive. With the natural simplicity and good taste of the upper classes, Alice was a master of the art of spending a fortune on things that were hardly noticeable.

A typical day in Alice's domestic life was dominated by a host of diverse duties. She would consult Monet when compiling the week's menus, at the same time taking account of the particular likes and dislikes of the lunch guests whose tastes she had noted. She had to arrange with the cook the matter of daily deliveries of vegetables from their kitchen-garden at the other end of the village.

Then there was the linen to be sorted out with Delphine, the maid, the curtains to arrange for her to iron, and some

An invisible barrier separated Alice and Monet's domain from the village. On one side of it, Giverny went about its business, while, on the other, Monet's home breathed to the rhythm and pace of the ancient ritual of cultivating the soil.

Alice ran the household, tolerated Monet's bad temper, brought up eight children

Opposite and above: The table laid for Sunday lunch. The blue Japanese-inspired china was used for most meals.

alterations being done by the seamstress to discuss with Delphine.

Alice also had to compile the shopping lists. Saturday was devoted to shopping. Sylvain would appear and take her to market at nearby Vernon. He himself was often given other tasks. He had to buy fresh bread and newspapers every day, run to a market-gardener who had a farm shop at Limetz to get some good asparagus, and search the watercress-farms of Saint-Marcel for that delicious watercress which features in the coat of arms of the town of Vernon. He might also need to buy some piece of kitchen equipment.

Alice had to remember to ask the floor-polisher to pay a visit. There was the store-room to restock, and the so-called spice-rack, a huge Régence-style cupboard stocked with the most precious preserves, tea from Kardomah, Salon de Provence olive oil, and spices such as cayenne pepper, saffron, paprika, cinnamon and cumin.

The morning would thus pass with lightning speed. It was always a surprise to hear the little train passing, such a useful device for regulating one's watch. The train was always on time even if, as often happened, it was delayed by their boys having hoisted the canoes on board to avoid having to pass through several locks. In any case, it was high time the boys were home, as Monet would be back at eleven, impatient to sit down to lunch and a demon for punctuality. A first then a second stroke of

Opposite: Claude Monet, *The Luncheon*, 1868. Frankfurt, Stadt Institut. The painting shows Camille and Jean at the table, with Monet's place in the foreground.

Below right: Monet photographed by Sacha Guitry.

Pages 56-57: The breakfast table. This meal was a hotchpotch of habits learned from trips to Britain and the Netherlands.

the gong would assemble the scattered family in the dining-room for lunch, which was served at 11.30 precisely. Monet would cough irritably on the very half-second, causing panic in the kitchen.

The reason the family lunched so early was to allow Monet to make the best use of the light to work on his afternoon subject. He had astonishing energy. Often rising before dawn, he would consult the weather-hill from his bedroom window, hoping to find it enveloped in a bluish haze, which would herald a fine day.

Next, he would take a cold bath – under the watchful eye of Cézanne's *Nègre*,

which hung in his dressing-room. He would then come down to the dining-room where a hearty breakfast awaited him. Monet would usually eat breakfast with Blanche, his step-daughter, who was also a painter, and who would enter with a wheelbarrow full of his canvases and easels for that day's subject. Then they were off through the countryside to the river to board their studio-boat, leaving the awakened house behind them, the day always full of little events to be recorded.

This first meal of the day was actually a hotchpotch of customs gleaned from trips to England and the Netherlands and, of course, from all those inns at which Monet

Above: Monet's desk as it might have looked in his lifetime.

Right: Monet, c. 1920, in the large studio, where he was painting the *Water-lily Decorations* panels for the Orangerie at the Tuilerie Gardens.

had stayed when he was painting in the countryside.

Familiar, happy sounds would emanate from the kitchen, where the oven was being lit, while they sat down to eggs and bacon, grilled tripe sausages and Dutch or Stilton cheese, with toast and orange marmalade and tea.

Fortunately, over the years, there were enough variations in the daily routine to shake the family out of this way it had of making time stand still.

As Monet had risen so early and worked from five or six o'clock in the morning, often in the wet, lunch at 11.30 was a welcome moment of relaxation which everyone found particularly important. It was also the meal to which guests were invited; the Monets never considered inviting people to dinner. This was largely because of the hour at which Monet retired. He would go to bed by 9.30 at the latest to be fresh for the next day's work. If he had to go any later, he would be completely out of sorts. In fact, in one of his letters, he recounts, as if he were talking about a major disaster, that he had to dine at ten o'clock at night after going to hear his friend, the poet Maurice Rollinat, sing in the church at Fresselines.

A table laid with the attractive blue china and the prospect of a good lunch would put him in a charming frame of mind – except on the days when he was dissatisfied with his painting! The family would often discreetly observe the way in which he entered the house and try to judge from his gait whether he was in a good temper.

In general, it was safest to serve food that was nothing less than delicious. Monet was such a fanatic about the right time for picking the vegetables that he would terrorise Florimond and his acolytes, and he could even burst into a rage over a sauce. Curiously, he would never reprimand the cook but would charge the mistress of the house with doing so.

This dining-room, in which the family portraits adorning the walls had been replaced by coloured Japanese woodcuts of landscapes and figures, was the scene for some incidents which sometimes smacked of the burlesque. For instance, there was the tragi-comical day when Marguerite made a mistake in her banana ice-cream recipe, and realised at the last moment that she was about to serve an ice-cream flavoured with kitchen salt. Everyone had a good laugh over it – 20 years later!

Like everyone else, Monet had his particular habits and preferences, as well as some rather interesting peculiarities.

For instance, although Paul would serve at table in his striped waistcoat, Monet revived a very ancient custom – one which had been taken very seriously by the gastronome Grimaud de la Reynière. He would carve the meat himself, at table, cutting up any kind of game, poultry or roast. For duck, he perfected a ceremony of his own devising. He would remove the wings, sprinkle them with nutmeg, freshly ground pepper and coarse salt and hand them over to Paul, who would take them into the kitchen to grill under the hottest flame imaginable.

As for salads, whether they were of endive laced with garlic and croutons or dandelions with strips of fat bacon or purslane, Paul would present him with the large serving-spoon which he would fill with freshly ground pepper and coarse salt and dip in olive oil, adding a drop or two of wine vinegar. Paul would then pour the contents of the spoon over the salad and toss it. It would be black with pepper and inedible for anyone except Monet or Blanche, who loved anything that he did. That is why there were always two bowls of salad. The same applied to asparagus, which he liked barely cooked: two separate dishes were needed.

In the wine-cellar, which was run by

Above: Monet liked to add a whole spoonful of pepper and salt to a salad, so there was one bowl for him and Blanche, and another for everyone else.

Opposite: The house glimpsed through the trees.

Pages 62-63: The Sunday lunch table. Lunch began at exactly 11.30 a.m. every day.

Sylvain, the local plonk was banned. Although Monet did not regard himself as a wine connoisseur, he did like fine wines, such as the burgundy recommended by Pissarro or the claret discovered by Durand-Ruel. He did not, however, disdain the minor vintages of the Loire and the rather harsh Chanturgue wine in which red kidney beans were cooked. Monet cared little for champagne, which, at his table, was served decanted like ordinary wine.

After dinner, coffee was served in the studio drawing-room, after which the family devoted itself to the ritual of the home-made plum brandy poured into little round glasses which had been brought back from Norway. A few other bottles lined the little glass-fronted cabinet – home-made blackcurrant wine, marc (white brandy) brought from his native Berry by Paul and, for the ladies, exotic liqueurs from the French colonies (which were as often as not manufactured in Bordeaux).

Monet never lingered over his food. The service was quick and he even gave the order never to hand dishes around twice when his American step-son-in-law, Theodore Butler, was lunching with them, since his slow eating habits drove Monet mad.

After the meal, Alice and her daughters would withdraw to the mauve drawing-room, which was also the library. Monet would go back to work until the two strokes of the gong interrupted him for seven-o'clock dinner.

Picnics and Celebration Lunches

*'From the car, one barely has the leisure to
compare different types of foliage. And one cannot
see the flowering hedgerows ... The trees that fly
away, they are trees, nothing more ... they gallop by.'*

MIRBEAU, *THE 628-E8*

Above: Traditional fare at the picnic marking the opening of the hunting season included pâtés *en croute* and terrines.

Opposite: A full lunch table, complete with glasses for the wine, was laid in the open air for the family's numerous picnics.

Little by little, even if their spirit lingers on, things change. There was the garden in which Monet worked so unstintingly and which he landscaped so brilliantly. There were the picnic baskets and the secret ritual of picking morels, the hunting parties and the trips to Paris. There was the arrival of Caillebotte or Mirbeau who had come by boat down the Seine, and, of course, the steady stream of visitors as the summer progressed. They would manage to penetrate the barrier that had to be built around Monet to protect his work. Yet all this gradually dissolved and metamorphosed.

The household – which was run to the rhythm of its own seasons, punctuated with exhibitions of Monet's work – saw the children grow up and marry, and eventually saw the serenity of its garden disturbed by the games of four grandchildren. With the turn of the century, the time came for walks with Lily, Suzanne's daughter (who became Jean-Marie Toulgouat's mother) in the cart drawn by the nanny-goat. The garden was filled with the sounds of children, the roaring of Lily's brother Jim's toy tigers, the wailing of the dolls owned by Germaine's daughters Sisi and Nitou; there were thirty-second crises and peals of laughter.

A second studio was therefore built near the lime-trees, just as a third studio would be erected in 1916 at the opposite end of the property.

A garage was built next to the bicycle shed, which was cluttered with a whole arsenal of fishing-rods and nets of every

65

kind – shrimping-nets, nets for holding big fish and double-meshed nets for catching eels in the River Rû. The garage, which even had a pit, was for Michel and Jean-Pierre, who loved to invent various pieces of diabolical, clanking machinery.

Gradually, motor-cars replaced the carriages bringing visitors to and from the Hotel Baudy, the café which had become a hotel to cater for the increasing number of artists making pilgrimages to Giverny.

Monet never took the trouble to learn to ride a horse or a bicycle, much less to drive a car, but the two boys delightedly interpreted the moods and rumblings of the engine of the family's first Panhard-Levassor, which would change so many of their habits. It is difficult to imagine today the fever which gripped the family when they visited the earliest Paris car shows. The first Panhard was followed by another and joined by the Bonnet-Zédel and the boys' Hotchkiss. Then there was that wonderful Zebra, the van which Sylvain used for going shopping. The day was still far off when the garage would house Michel's off-road vehicle, which was specially designed for crossing the Sahara.

The Abbé Toussaint officiated at the marriage ceremony of another of Alice's children, Suzanne. The household would

Pages 66-67: The basket contains ceps, chanterelles and oyster mushrooms. A mushroom-picking foray was an excellent excuse for a picnic.

henceforth include an American son-in-law (Jean-Marie's grandfather) as well as a Norwegian daughter-in-law (Jacques's wife). It was also about to encompass a son-in-law (Germaine's husband) from Monaco and another daughter-in-law (Jean-Pierre's wife) from Périgord. After the ceremony, there was a luncheon, the menu for which has been preserved; it was served in the studio-drawing-room. Four rows of paintings overlooked the guests as they dined. The rest of the day was spent in conversation around the pond. On this day of all days, nothing would induce one to forget to feed the goldfish.

Following the Monet-Rodin exhibition of 1889 at Georges Petit's gallery, the names of these two artists were on everyone's lips, and the family was able to enjoy a more affluent lifestyle.

The famous exclamation of their friend, Georges de Bellio, 'Et maintenant vive Monet! Vive Rodin! (For ever Monet! For ever Rodin!) Hurrah!' had launched an era of true prosperity and sounded the knell on that terrible period of unpaid bills.

Thus, by 1901, five gardeners were working in the garden which luxuriated in a deceptive simplicity, while another was employed solely to look after the pond which Monet had had dug several years earlier, and which he was about to have enlarged.

In the previous year, he had exhibited landscapes inspired by this water-garden at

Durand-Ruel's gallery. Now, in 1903, he was preparing for his first exhibition at the Bernheim brothers' gallery. This would for ever change his relationship to money: his paintings would have a nought added to the price with remarkable regularity until by 1910 they were costing an average of 12,000 francs per canvas. The time was approaching when *Women in the Garden,* rejected for exhibition at the official Salon in 1867, would sell for 20,000 francs.

During this period, Monet's presence at Giverny attracted a lot of people, and this sleepy, peasant village found itself home to a colony of American artists. Some of them lived at the café-cum-grocery which had become the delightful Hotel Baudy. It was here that they drank neat spirits and played the piano or the banjo until late at night. Others rented or bought houses in which they led an active, and often sophisticated, social life. They held at-homes, garden parties, and soirées, at which they wore camellia buttonholes. The guest lists included many Americans living in Paris.

The painters who asked for lessons and others who sought an invitation out of simple curiosity had to be politely but firmly turned away. All this led Monet to isolate himself even further.

The years slipped by, each using up its store of simple pleasures and complicated troubles, dominated by a very full calendar of wonderful meals. Between the ordinary days and the days on which there were

Below: Two group photos of the family gathered for the picnics that were always held to celebrate the hunting season. Monet didn't hunt but he loved game.

guests, there were the Sunday family lunches, and the celebration lunches on June 6, Monet's saint's day, and November 14, Monet's birthday. Then, of course, there were the Christmas and New Year's lunches, in addition to the ceremonial picnics which were not to be missed for anything, especially the one held to mark the opening of the hunting season.

Pages 70-71: During the hunting season, the picnic trestle table would be set up on the hillside in the shade of an apple tree.

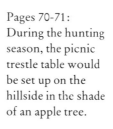

Above: Claude
Monet, *Luncheon*,
c. 1873, Musée du
Louvre, Paris.

Opposite: Claude
Monet, *Luncheon
on the Grass*
(central fragment),
1865-1866. Paris,
Musée d'Orsay.

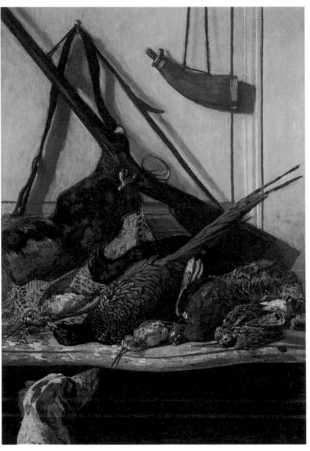

Marguerite reigned and tormented herself in the blue kitchen overlooking the garden. From mid-April, she could watch the flowering of two Japanese apple trees, which produced a wealth of pink-and-white blossoms. She was surrounded by all her pans, pots, casseroles and copper fish-kettles, her baking sheets for meringues, her strings of moulds, and the country stove for baking her apple tarts. There were strainers and sieves, earthenware dishes – which she called stone dishes – for baking a red fruit pie, along with the weighing scales, the ancient ice-cream

Above: Claude Monet, *Hunting Trophies*, 1862, Paris. Musée d'Orsay.

maker, and the nutmeg grater. Marguerite had an enormous amount of work, even when helped by first one, and later two, kitchen-maids.

Once the kitchen-garden vegetables had been delivered very early in the morning, she would prepare a hot first course for luncheon. Then there would be a meat or fish dish, sometimes both, a hot vegetable, a salad and a different dessert every day, as well as cakes for teatime.

The evening meal began with soup – dinner without soup would have been inconceivable – and this was followed by an egg or cheese dish, such as individual soufflés served in ramekins. Then would come the main course, or *plat de résistance*, which might be poultry, a gratin dish or cold meat, plus a salad and cheese. No special dessert was made for dinner. Either dessert left over from lunch would be finished, or one of Marguerite's compotes – cherries, plums, or peaches preserved in their own juice – would be served. No one could make them like Marguerite; she would serve them with a biscuit or a piece of sponge cake.

Monet liked his chicory, French beans and even chestnuts steamed. He also insisted on having his spinach cooked 'in hardly any water' to preserve the flavour and colour. He liked ceps (wild mushrooms) in olive oil; according to the family, this was the only recipe which he could claim to have invented. He often demanded guinea-fowl, which could only be bought from Ledanois.

All this would have driven any household mad. The worst moment of all was when an art dealer announced he was about to pay a call. According to season, the hunters in the family would be warned that the best game was required, or the best pike, for which Monet would have to pay dearly – even if he bought it from the gardener, who would have netted it from a boat in Monet's own pond. Or Sylvain might be sent out to buy turbot or the almost legendary monkfish.

The ceremony of selecting Florimond's tiniest vegetables would add to this disruption of the household, because everything had to be perfect for Messrs. Durand-Ruel or Bernheim, to say nothing of Thadée Natanson, in whose honour two ducks would be served, or Whistler, who was given pigeon stew. Theodore Butler (Suzanne's American husband who, after her tragic death in 1899, married Marthe) would be served with lobster Newburg, prepared from the Delmonico's, New York recipe. He was also treated to Welsh rarebit and the red cabbage which reminded him of Pennsylvania red cabbage. Each of the sons- and daughters-in-law brought their own customs and tastes with them.

To add to the difficulties, if the guest happened to be someone whom the boys judged to be boring, Alice or Blanche had to request picnic baskets for them. The boys were so used to their plant and insect collections that they would describe visitors whom they did not like in entomological terms.

It was not uncommon, after the Monets had had guests or taken a trip to Paris, for the cook to find herself presented with a new recipe which must be attempted, while following the instructions most closely. It is tantalising to conjecture about what happened to the recipe for fillet of sole Marguéry, or to wonder how Marguerite could cook from another indecipherable recipe presented by Maupassant.

After one of Monet's trips to London, Marguerite had to learn to make Yorkshire pudding as served at the Savoy Hotel. It is not known why Madame Renoir's famous *bouillabaisse* does not appear in the notebooks; perhaps some of the ingredients were unobtainable at Giverny.

On the other hand, three recipes provided by the Guitry family were included in the book – Sacha's shoulder of pork, Lucien Guitry's lamb stew and Charlotte Lysès's stuffed white onions. Charlotte Lysès was a very famous actress of the period; she was Sacha's first wife and was adored by the whole family. Millet's recipe for bread rolls appears after Mallarmé's recipe for chanterelle mushrooms, Cézanne's salt cod soup, and lobster American-style from Drouant's. There are Foyot pork chops from the restaurant of the same name, oxtail stew from Marguéry's, Florentine fillets of sole from the Café de Paris, Julien's brill Dugléré-style, and of course upside down apple tart from the Tatin sisters.

It is easy to see why women who have cooked for the famous have made their names. Clemenceau had his Marie in the Rue Franklin, Dumas had his own Marie and Degas his Zoé. Thus, in Monet's household, after Rita, Caroline, and Melanie, there could only be Marguerite.

As often happens when the household routine is of paramount importance, there was little difference between ordinary days and those on which guests were invited. The menus may have been chosen a little more carefully to allow for the tastes of the visitors, but the table was set just as attractively for everyday. The tablecloths were always yellow and only two sets of tableware were ever used. These were the underglaze blue Creil earthenware of the pattern called Japon, with its stylised dark-blue cherry-trees and fans, and the white porcelain service with the wide yellow border and blue edging reserved for special days and important guests. The table centrepiece consisted of little bouquets of flowers from the garden or greenhouse, tiny honey-coloured orchids and bee-orchids, wild flowers or clematis floating in plain bowls. It had to look completely uncontrived.

Two cabinets from the Pays de Caux in Normandy displayed the family silver – soup tureens, tankards, chocolate pots, and coffee pots, while next to a pyramid of fruits and the decanters stood the big silver samovar for tea.

Dishes were served elegantly in the Monet household but were not given elaborate names or garnishes.

It is a matter of great regret that the everyday menus were never written down. If only Monet had taken a leaf from Whistler's book – it was Whistler's custom not only to write them down but also to decorate them with a little drawing, before autographing them with his famous Japanese-style butterfly monogram.

Opposite: Baked peaches fresh from the oven, one of the traditional Sunday desserts (recipe on page 166).

It was in this setting of chrome yellow furniture and walls, and among Monet's superb collection of Japanese prints, that the celebratory lunches took place. Such was the lunch held each year on November 14, Monet's birthday.

Before it took place, the male members of the family would vie for the honour of killing the woodcock, or several if possible, for the occasion. But it was Jean-Pierre, the best shot, who became the official purveyor of the delicacy. Unlike other game, woodcock does not spoil, and those who like it prefer it well-hung, though perhaps not to the point which Monet did. It was left to hang for 14 days in the cellar, then plucked and roasted.

Paul, the butler, would present it at table, accompanied by a large slice of bread. Monet would remove the innards, spread them on the bread, and eat it. This was quite

Above: On Christmas Day the famous truffled foie gras pâté ordered from Strasbourg was one of the delicacies served.

the normal way to treat small feathered game, such as thrush with juniper berries, but in the case of woodcock the gizzard was generally first removed and discarded. For this birthday lunch, the woodcock had to be home-caught; on that day, game was never bought from the dealer.

Apart from the woodcock, two other dishes were customarily served, a large fish – pike or turbot – and the *vert-vert*, a dessert that looked as good as it tasted. This was a cake flavoured with pistachio and iced with glistening green fondant, as exotic as something out of an oriental fairy-tale. The rest of the meal varied according to the year and the inspiration of the moment.

In this household which had experienced so many rituals and clearly marked seasons, the most magnificent meal, as for most families, was the Christmas lunch.

For once, they dined at midday. The

dining-room was bedecked with simple garlands of leaves and flowers, and the best crystal and silverware were laid out on the best tablecloth with the yellow dishes. The bowls in the centre of the table held clusters of white viburnum, Christmas roses and jasmine. The children would find at their places those little grey envelopes lined with rose madder, containing a sum of money from La Bonne (short for 'La Bonne Maman' or grandmother) and from Monet. Next to the napkins, there were mysterious little packets of sweets and small gifts – pins, medallions, and fob watches. The large presents were waiting under the tree which had been installed in the mauve drawing-room.

For Christmas lunches, an old custom was revived, one which had survived from the days when a strict caste system ruled the farmyard. The goose had been placed at the bottom of the social scale and chicken was at the top, though only capons and fatted hens were deemed worthy to appear at a good table.

The menu began with eggs scrambled with truffles, or monkfish cooked American-style. Traditionally, Strasbourg truffled foie gras in pastry was served before the truffled, stuffed capons were presented on a bed of chestnuts and Périgord truffles, served with a chestnut purée. A light salad of lamb's lettuce would offset the heaviness of these dishes, followed by a Roquefort or Gorgonzola cheese. Finally, there came that moment which constituted the true magic of Christmas for the children. Paul would close the shutters and bring in the Christmas pudding, over which a generous measure of rum had been poured. He would strike a match and set light to the pudding, to the great joy of all present, who would exclaim in admiration. The crystal decanters containing wine and champagne would suddenly shine with greater brilliance.

To complete the festivities, home-made banana ice-cream from the reliable old ice-cream maker would make its appearance, looking like a sugar-loaf. As usual, coffee would be served in the studio-drawing-room, followed by the brandies and liqueurs.

The next day's lunch at Marthe and Theodore Butler's was just as gargantuan, but the cheese came after the pudding.

With time, as they married off, the family became rather scattered, but a celebration would soon bring them together again. Reunions around a well-stocked table or a lunch served outdoors strengthened the ties between.

Thus, the first sunny days would find them packing picnic-hampers into their boats or cars, opening the picnicking season which was strung out throughout the year. There was the Mascaret picnic, the Côte de Gaillon Racetrack picnic, the Paris-Madrid Road Race picnic, and many others which had not been endowed with

Pages 80-87: The garden and house in mid-winter. Everyone was preparing to celebrate Christmas. By their places at the table, the children would find the famous 'little packets' – those little pale-grey envelopes containing a sum of money – as well as mysterious little boxes of goodies.

Opposite and above: Christmas was the main festival to which Marguerite's cuisine made a major contribution in the form of sweets, chocolates and cakes. All these goodies were accompanied by large quantities of Veuve Clicquot champagne.

special names. The family would bring along a few close friends such as Pierre and Jean Sisley, Lucien Pissarro, Fernand Haundorf, the young Perry girls and Germain Raingo, one of the few cousins admitted to this kind of outing. The rest were so indescribably chic and conventional that they couldn't possibly be taken along.

*I*n fact, once the good weather had come, one picnic followed another, worthy descendants of those very first lunches al fresco in the garden when Monet, Alice, and their eight children had just arrived, so many years before. Those lunches had been eaten under a sort of awning improvised from straw matting. The memories of them were a pleasant reminder of the first days spent at Giverny, when thousands of plans were being hatched, in the excitement of having finally found a true home.

For numerous reasons, visitors to Monet's home were usually invited to a meal, but obviously most of the guests were more interested in Monet's painting and his ideas for a garden, than in a meal outdoors which could, in fact, have been eaten anywhere. It is surprising how many people love the countryside, but prefer to look at it through a drawing-room window, from a hotel terrace or through a car windscreen.

There is a big difference between strolling along the little paths of the water garden or crossing the Japanese bridge, and venturing, basket in hand, into the forest to look for wild mushrooms. After such an excursion, one drops down on to a plaid rug to lunch on the ground, throwing one's hat into the bushes and breathing in the damp air of the undergrowth, before returning to a car which stands in a cloud of insolent mosquitoes and whose coughing engine refuses to start.

Alice loved the garden, the pond and the beauty of the countryside but no one ever saw her with secateurs or watering can in hand. She could be found with a cup of tea, working on something, or reading on the balcony and contemplating the garden below. On the other hand, she was the first to leap into the motor-car for any sort of outing.

The hunting season was the time for a family migration, including all the cousins who had come to stay in neighbouring houses. Some came from the Vendée, others from Cagnes or Rouen. All were experienced hunters, including the women. They would set off early in the morning, with beaters and hare-coursers, armed with shotguns and blunderbusses, and return exhausted at lunchtime, to be feted with the sacrosanct picnic which marked the opening of the season. Baskets and hampers of victuals had been packed into the cars, together with trestles and chairs. The folding table was set up on the hillside, under a spreading apple tree, where it awaited the heroes of the day.

Monet did not hunt but he adored game, especially partridge, and he was even fonder of woodcock. This did not stop him from often intoning, at the sight of the pâtés *en croute* and the terrines of wild rabbit and duck, which were the traditional menu for that day: 'Come eat, eat, let us eat this pigeon which will only be good if it is eaten hot.' The luncheon, during which the hunters regaled the company with their usual exaggerations, ended with fruit tarts, fresh fruit and praise for the various bottles of cider and wine. This was one of the last such lunches of the year when the weather was good. Although July and August were frequently wet, September was usually a fine month at Giverny.

The family did a great deal of driving – the speed bug had bitten them – and even Monet would not for the world have missed the picnic held to watch the Paris-Madrid Rally go by in the Beauce plain. He was even more enthusiastic about the Côte de Gaillon Race. Thenceforward, the nearest forests were abandoned in favour of others further afield from which they would bring back baskets full of ceps. Anything was a good excuse for an excursion and a picnic. Monet would even let himself go, to the extent of singing, 'Espoir charmant, Sylvain m'a dit, je t'aime'. ('Delightful hope, Sylvain said to me, I love you', a popular song.) Sylvain organised

Pages 92-93: The yellow-bordered porcelain with the blue edging was only used for special occasions and for distinguished guests.

and led the expeditions to visit the Tatin sisters, to sample several of their famous apple tarts at La Mothe-Beuvron.

In the village of Giverny, truly good food was important to a lot of people. At the inn, Madame Baudy would try to please her American guests by preparing Boston baked beans and stuffed spareribs, while all the young artists would sing the praises of squash and the Philadelphia pepper pot which, so they said, had helped the troops of a general who was unknown in Giverny to win a battle no one had ever heard of. This fact did not stop them from forgetting their sorrows in a waltz or a cakewalk.

For the servants, the days were busy and very long. Like many domestics at that time, they had only the vaguest notions of leisure. In the noble tradition of families of grooms from the Sologne region, Sylvain would relax in the evenings by playing the hunting horn in the garden. Marguerite, instead of dreaming of some tranquil shore, would sit perched on her rocking-chair absorbed in a cookery book, such as *Pot-au-Feu* or *Luculle*.

In the meantime, in the mauve drawing-room, people would be reading old-fashioned, impracticable recipes. The next menu would be discussed while browsing through a catalogue from the publisher Charpentier, or embroidering while sucking sweets from Fouquet, bergamot oranges candied in honey, or violet bon-bons from Paris. The menu would certainly

not be composed for its health-giving pow-ers. In this household, it was inadvisable to admit to being indifferent to good food. Nothing could be more suspect; one would soon be taxed with philistinism, and be treated with a hint of condescension.

There would be few recipes here of the invalid beef-tea type, nor any of those Lenten menus, which were treated with what could be called Alice's bigotry. No one would think of dieting, although one might toy with the idea of a homeopathic remedy, such as the one prescribed by J. Prost-Lacuzon, and prepared by the famous Georges Weber pharmacy in the Rue des Capucines, for Alice. It left no doubt as to her preoccupations: 'Arseni-cum, Sulphur, Calc. carb. (Calcarea Carbo-nica), Iodium, to be taken in alternate weeks. Follow a diet, increase the amount of exercise, lead a very active life, etc...'

At the slightest indisposition, one could rush to consult the book of medicinal remedies. This would be followed by a raid on Florimond's kitchen-garden for a few leaves of melissa, alpine mint, or even borage to soothe coughing on cold nights, although tea made from violet flowers had a more delicate flavour.

This book of medicinal remedies – which advised on the treatment of chlorosis in young girls, fevers of all kinds, and excessive eating – contained a chapter on mental illnesses, and particularly misan-thropy, which was to be combatted by

taking five different preparations in 12th and 13th dilutions.

A day had to be arranged on which to invite those cousins whom one wouldn't dare take on a picnic because they were so elegant and starchy, and who seemed to treat the Monets like friendly natives. Aunt Cécile Rémy, whose majesty appeared as though it would crush the whole garden, was the very image of Aunt Marguerite Le Moyne. In fact, all the aunts and cousins wanted to see for themselves what a successful painter looked like, but it is never much fun for those who are being stared at like animals at the zoo. Of course, the guests were delighted: Monsieur Monet was famous.

In the very small room, the children spoke more openly of Ernest Hoschedé, whose image still floated before them, as they leafed through copies of *Art et La Mode*, which he had founded and in which Stéphane Mallarmé had published his 'White Waterlily'.

Yet the atmosphere was not gloomy in the mauve drawing-room – which res-embled an aviary most of the time. Monet had been quite right to remove his studio to the other end of the garden and allow no one inside without his permission. Only Alice was admitted. She would sit there embroidering, sewing and talking about painting to Monet. Later, Blanche took her place.

In that little mauve drawing-room one could admit to liking Maxime du Camp, not understanding Ibsen, and detesting Zola or Barrès. Russian novels and the stories of Turgenev were devoured enthusiastically, as were the poems of Mallarmé, his wonderful letters, and his stories, which were just as interesting. There was much discussion of the latest news of the fire at the Opéra-Comique, and of La Tarasque who was going north from the Rhone Valley to settle in Paris.

Monet travelled almost every year, and wrote home every day. After much persuasion from his family, in his letters from London he described in greater detail than usual the grand occasions he attended, even describing such aspects as the dresses worn at them, for the benefit of his daughters-in-law who would have loved to have joined him.

John Singer Sargent usually organised Monet's trips, whisking him through a whirlwind of dinners in town. He introduced Monet to curators, collectors, Princess Louise and the London world of art and politics. He even took him to view the grandiose spectacle of Queen Victoria's funeral, which he watched from the window of a friend's house. This was the day on which Monet made the acquaintance of Henry James. At this time, London was a more exciting place than Paris. There was,

for instance, the Bath Club in Dover Street where half of Europe took a dip before going to immerse themselves in the calmer waters of Carlsbad. To someone living in the country, the London chronicles and the trips to Paris, like visits from friends, were indispensible for preventing the most fatal intellectual lethargy.

Of course, matters were not always so simple, especially when Monet, who was always courteous towards his guests, made a scene or declined one of the exciting invitations with which he was bombarded – for example, staying with the Potter-Palmers in Chicago or at the Palazzo Barbaro with Mary Hunter, visiting Mrs. Sargent Curtis, or travelling to Japan or even India.

Below: Monet was fond of chestnuts, but he liked them steamed. They were served in a variety of dishes.

Birds of Passage

*'Run away to a village to make it
the centre of the world.'*

JULES RENARD, *DIARY*.

Above: Claude Monet, *The Cakes (Les Galettes)*, 1882, private collection, Paris.

Opposite: Tea was served in the garden whenever the weather permitted. Monet liked strong tea, which came from the Kardomah shop.

Monet, who was so demanding, who had his work and adored comfort and good food, also loved nature to a degree rarely found in a town-dweller. In him, qualities that would in most people be in conflict were reconciled. He was simultaneously a bourgeois and a countryman, a bon viveur and an ascetic.

For Alice, life was not so simple, and this fundamental difference between the two of them was noticeable. Although she shared all of Monet's interests, he would retreat into his work totally absorbed, leaving her with a prospect of emptiness. This was especially the case on those long winter days he often chose for his painting campaigns, and whole months would go by when he would not hold a proper conversation with anyone at all. Yet Alice was in her element when surrounded by friends. For her, the regular trips to Paris were almost certainly as vital as the migrations of those birds of passage who landed in the garden at Giverny.

Vernon, the neighbouring town where the family shopped, had caught up with the times, and it was now possible to buy numerous delicacies there: Ceylon, Darjeeling or China teas, Italian cheeses from Paris, as well as clothing, sweets from Fouquet, visiting cards, leather, chintz and cretonne for the day-beds in the studios.

When the Monets went to Paris on shopping trips, or to meet a dealer, organise an exhibition, dine with friends or see a show, they would either take the train to the Saint-Lazare railway station or go by car. Sylvain, who was frightened of driving in town, would drop them at the Porte de Saint-Cloud. They would stay at the Hotel Terminus, which served as the head-quarters for the whole family, especially Butler and Marthe, and later Jim and Lily, Butler's children from his marriage to Suzanne. Remaining on the right bank of the Seine, they would hurry to the great buildings designed by Hausmann in which the art galleries had taken root. Here the Monets' passions for art and for good food could both be indulged with ease.

For their restaurants, they would actually visit relatively few arrondissements. They would wander between the Seine and what was then called the Boulevard, between Saint-Augustin and the Alexander III Bridge, from the Place de l'Europe to the Tuileries gardens, between the Passage du Havre, the Passage Choiseul and the Passage des Panoramas, between Marigny and the Faubourg Saint-Denis.

Their trips were timed to coincide with the Salons and the Universal Exhibitions. Although their sons frequented the races at the Vélodrome and visited the shows at the Palais de l'Automobile and the botanical gardens, they themselves would frequent a more literary side of Paris. Their most daring excursions were to visit the theatres. They often attended opening nights of plays, especially those of their good friend, Mirbeau. They also went to see their actor friends such as Coquelin in *Le Bourgeois Gentilhomme*, Lucien Guitry in *Chantecler*, Eve Lavallière at the Théâtre des Variétés and Mademoiselle Després at the Théâtre Antoine in *Poil de Carotte*. Naturally, they were familiar with the almost inexhaustible list of music-halls. At about this time, Paris was listening to the sayings of Alphonse Allais, Courteline's jokes, Tristan Bernard's wit and the still incomprehensible ideas of Alfred Jarry.

They listened to Rose Caron, a great interpreter of Wagner's music, and to Chaliapine in *Boris Godunov* and went to the Folies Bergères to watch Loïe Fuller (presented by the sculptor, Rodin) performing her snake-dance. Then there were the Javanese dancers and those from the Cambodian Ballet Royal. They heralded the arrival of the Ballets Russes, directed by Diaghilev, that tornado of a man, with scenery by Bakst and the scandalous *L'Après-midi d'un Faune* danced by Nijinsky. Most unexpected was Alice's taste for wrestling matches which were extremely violent.

The pace was fast: one show a day, a different restaurant each evening or dinner with friends. Clearly, even if one tried to avoid excessive noise and bustle, Paris was not to be visited with impunity.

Monet had instituted their Friday Dîner Drouant, and on the first Thursday of each month, Mallarmé, Georges de Bellio, Caillebotte and Renoir would meet at the Café Riche. They had set up so many dinners

With regard to the restaurants patronised by the Monets, those untypical times were long past when Monet had preferred a simple stew, eating in places frequented by emaciated young men wearing voluminous greatcoats, who seemed to live on a diet of milk and aphorisms. It was a long time since the art critic Geffroy and

Above: June, 1921. Monet standing with Clemenceau and Lily on the Japanese bridge.

and meetings of one group or another that it was impossible to keep up the pace.

The name has been lost of the restaurant at which Monet and Antonin Proust dined after their seconds had dissuaded them from fighting a duel. The custom of the day was to go to Ledoyen after having fought bravely in the Bois de Boulogne; this had also been the headquarters of Ernest Hoschedé after his visits to the Salons. In the 1900s, Monet and Alice would dine at Prunier's, Julien's, the Café de Paris, the Café Anglais, or Marguéry's, always choosing dishes that were not served at Giverny.

At Drouant, they would dine with Eugène Carrière, Rodin, Ajalbert, Lucien Descaves, Maurice Joyant, Rosny, Clemenceau, Coquelin, Frantz Jourdain and Edmond de Goncourt. After eating their woodcock Drouant-style, or brill in red wine, it was the custom to order Josette pears which absolutely had to be accompanied by an Haut-Brion wine reserved for the occasion by Drouant himself. Goncourt would wax lyrical at these Friday dinners and speak nostalgically of crayfish butter which had been invented in his native Lorraine (lost to France in the Franco-Prussian War, but restored to her in 1918).

All these famous personalities who used to meet in Paris would hurry down to Giverny at the first opportunity, hardly waiting to be asked. Naturally, they wanted to come in the summer to see the gardens, and Alice was kept busy organising this horde of visitors. She had to make endless arrangements and deal with every sort of interruption. It was very difficult, even unthinkable, not to accede to the requests of admirers who had been recommended by a dealer or a friend. When Monet was engrossed in his work, it meant he had to stop and tidy his studio, causing a complete break in that demanding schedule of creativity in its pure state. It also meant taking the risk of displeasing someone who might become a collector.

Yet Alice enjoyed having guests, especially as Monet's friends were never boring or colourless. Of course, there were a few fashionable people who were rather too gossipy and who would talk a load of nonsense just to make themselves sound amusing; the wife of a certain painter had to be tolerated despite the stories she was capable of inventing. But that sort of person was soon overwhelmed by all the others.

Curiously, Monet, who had always tried to keep his prices high, even in his most difficult times, and had refused to allow any dealer exclusive rights, managed to maintain a friendship based on a business relationship with both the Bernheim brothers and with Durand-Ruel. However, things did not always go well, especially as this house was not exactly full of people noted for their diplomacy.

Alice, who had retained a talent for spending the housekeeping money agreeably, left over from the days when she lived in splendour, knew better than anyone how important it was to treat the dealers properly.

Alice received her guests in a house smothered under young vines and roses,

Above: Monet and his friend the horticulturist, Georges Truffaut, examining the Japanese peonies in the garden at Giverny.

surrounded by a garden in which the seasons appeared as a succession of different beautifully controlled harmonies. The colour scheme changed from crimson, softened by banks of pink or white, to the bronze tide of late August, giving way to the blues and mauves of autumn.

This walled universe increased the impression of isolation and serenity, and few would have dared to arrive unannounced to disturb Monet. Sacha Guitry, who thought this rule did not apply to him, found himself forced to go on his way.

Friends from Paris were joined by those from London and Venice, as well as Americans, mainly from the east coast and Chicago. The only local resident who visited was the Abbé Toussaint, converted to cosmopolitanism by the force of events. He spoke English quite well.

Otherwise they came from all over, taking the train at the Saint-Lazare station for Vernon, where a car had been ordered to meet them. A few stalwarts preferred to walk from there. The most fashionable people came by boat down the Seine; these included Caillebotte, Mirbeau, the Depeaux, the Helleus, the Johnstons and many others. They abandoned their hotels, houses and overdecorated flats to relax in this rural setting. Here, they would lunch in very simple; though ultra-modern surroundings, accentuated here and there by a piece of Delft earthenware or an Arita vase, or by the blue and coppery sheen of an Imari vase, or even a discreet East India

Company epergne, one of the rare pieces of 'famille rose' porcelain to have escaped the horrors of the public auctions at Rottenbourg.

It was customary for guests to arrive in the late morning to lunch at 11.30, after viewing the latest paintings in the studio and paying a short visit to the greenhouses. Conversation became animated between the time when the coffee was served in the drawing-room and teatime. Tea was served under the lime-trees, on the balcony or near the pond. Sometimes people would climb the stairs to look at Monet's private collection of paintings by Cézanne, Renoir, Pissarro, Degas, Morisot, Manet, Signac, Corot and Delacroix. The display never included all the paintings and would frequently be changed.

At teatime, Paul would bring in the boiling water, and Alice, or later Blanche, would dole out teaspoons of the precious tea-leaves from Kardomah; scones, chestnut biscuits or cinnamon toast would be served.

Everyone knew how strictly Monet kept to his timetable. He hated visitors to use their own transport because they would always be late, or get lost on the way, or have one, two or even three breakdowns. Marguerite once confided that one day she thought he would sit down at table without waiting for the guests, he was so annoyed at seeing his daily schedule disrupted.

So many people came here that it is impossible to list them all. Painter friends, such as Renoir, Sisley, Pissarro, and Cézanne, used to visit during the early, difficult days. Later, they were joined by other artists, such as Eugène Carrière, Paul Helleu, and John Singer Sargent. There were even a few artists from Giverny's American colony such as Lilla Cabot Perry, Theodore Robinson, and, obviously, Theodore Earl Butler, who had become one of the family through marriage. The Monets were very close friends with the Caillebottes, who had helped them at those very critical periods when they had no money, as well as with Berthe Morisot and Degas. A more distant relationship developed later with the American Impressionist, Mary Cassatt, and even later with Vuillard, K.X. Roussel and Pierre Bonnard. Even Matisse paid them one or two visits.

The numerous artists interested in Monet's work were joined by writers such as Stéphane Mallarmé or Paul Valéry as well as Georges Clemenceau, who understood the progress of the water-lily paintings very well and wrote about them in his books. Those who were most highly regarded by Monet and Alice were probably Mallarmé, Rodin, Marbeau, Clemenceau, Gustave Geffroy and certainly Durand-Ruel.

The dealer Maurice Joyant announced his visit with Isaac de Camondo to acquire *Cathedrals*, while Lucien Guitry wanted to bring Anatole France, which greatly pleased Monet. The Bernheims sent the Prince de Wagram, who drove so fast that they did not want to come down with him in his automobile.

Sacha Guitry and Charlotte Lysès were frequent visitors to Giverny as was Mary Hunter, a friend of Sargent. Fasquelle, Gallimard and Charpentier represented the world of publishing. Other welcome guests included Henry Farman, a British aviator who painted in his spare time, and the eccentric Whistler. Whistler would often receive his own guests in a sort of kimono; he would cook the meal himself and had no hesitation in colouring the food to match his underglaze blue dinner service.

Japanese influence, which was all the rage in the West, was to be found everywhere. Commodore Perry, who had first discovered Japan for the West, had a great-nephew living in Giverny.

There were Japanese woodcuts on the walls, Japanese pottery and vases, oiled paper sunshades, little wooden houses and a white porcelain figure of a sleeping cat, which was left on the sofa of the third studio to symbolise the fact that all cats were forbidden entry because they dug up the flowerbeds. There were all the books of woodcuts or translated stories presented as gifts by friends, not to mention the Japanese lily bulbs, so rare in France, which

were sent to Giverny from Japan. There were also items which were Japanese-inspired, like the Creil china, or the habit of embroidering initials or first names in a vertical arrangement. All this was, however, a far cry from the erudite bric-a-brac to be found at Edmond de Goncourt's home and which was exhibited in the annex to the Universal Exhibition. Anything unusual was dubbed 'Japanese'.

It is strange to find no trace of a special menu for the Japanese guests. The Kuroki family were among the first Japanese to visit Monet's house and buy paintings. Madame Kuroki was a close friend of Blanche; her grandmother, the Marchioness Matsukata, had been a member of the immediate entourage of the Empress.

Naturally, in their shuttling back and forth between Tokyo, Marseilles and Paris, the Kurokis had had much opportunity to become Westernised. They did so just enough to be able to tolerate the unæsthetic jumble of Western tastes, the food served ungarnished and the decorations displayed in such suffocating profusion. Monet and Alice knew that the Japanese of every era have liked sobriety, purity of line, and monochrome colour schemes. At Giverny, the Japanese were served with the white and yellow china with the blue edging, because the blue service, which was a French imitation of Japanese pottery, might have appeared to be some sort of practical joke by the manufacturer.

Other Japanese visitors, Monsieur Bing, Monsieur Hayashi and Monsieur Kazunori Ishibashi, who were all æsthetes, were reassured by the little Japanese inscription in blue, painted on a flower-block, which congratulated Monet on behalf of all Japan for having been one of the first painters in the West to have abandoned perspective. They also admired the Japanese pottery on the mantelpiece which was painted with a design of bats. What with these visitors, as well as such people as Bernard Berenson, Sir William Rothenstein, and a certain Mr. Calder (an artist himself and father of the sculptor Alexander Calder), Giverny could have been mistaken for a suburb of Boston or Yokohama!

The visitors represented the widest spectrum of political opinion. There were, for instance, both admirers and detractors of Victor Hugo. But this was no problem. The real problem of these luncheons, apart from the menus or the tastes and opinions of the guests, was the means of transporting them. Some preferred a horse and carriage, while others were addicted to speed.

Then there were the unpredictable moods of Degas. He was perfectly capable of making one die of laughter at his aphorisms, but only if everyone was in step with him. One couldn't invite him with Paul Helleu whom he had dubbed 'the steam Watteau'.

Lunches at Giverny posed many other problems. Too many very different people encountered each other there. The times were just too loaded with explosives. There was the day, for example, when Rodin found Cézanne on his knees before him in the garden thanking him for having shaken his hand. Cézanne, with his temperamental and hypersensitive nature, was prone to bizarre, unpredictable behaviour.

With Rodin there were innumerable subjects to avoid, such as his complicated love affairs which were public knowledge. Yet Rodin sent Giverny one of the most beautiful dancers ever, Isadora Duncan, who captivated the sons of the family. For Monet, Isadora danced as Nijinsky had danced for Rodin and Marguerite Namara from the Chicago Opera played the piano in Monet's large studio known as the Waterlily Studio.

As always, Clemenceau remained a close family friend, even though his involvement in the 1892 Panama Canal Company scandal put him in an extremely delicate position.

This was at the time when Clemenceau had become involved in a duel which made him a figure of fun. In the election the following year, Clemenceau was defeated. (Nine years later, however, he was re-elected, eventually to become Prime Minister once more.)

Life at Giverny for Monet included reading the works of Paul Valéry, plucking a faded iris head, and receiving the whole

Above: The Japanese bridge on a misty day.

world or at least a third of it. It was chatting to Delphine, who had come to deliver the starched linen, running off to London to grumble at the parliament building which was so impossible to paint and smoking those dreadful Caporal Rose cigarettes to the last days of his life.

The assassination of Archduke Ferdinand plunged the whole world into war. At Giverny, as elsewhere, life became sad, complicated and much altered. Yet nothing totally interrupted the established rituals. There were the lunches with the Goncourt academicians in the Large Studio; the lunch with Clemenceau on November 14, 1918, in honour of Monet's birthday, three days after the Armistice; and the last great post-war lunches with the Kurokis.

Monet died in 1926 and Blanche, who had replaced her mother as mistress of the household after 1911, continued against all

Pages 106-107: Monet treated champagne like any other white wine and decanted it into a carafe for serving.

odds. Truly, when a Hoschedé-Monet was involved, there was no question of sinking into the habit of one-course meals and processed food .

Many years later, in September 1940, when the established order was once again upset, Blanche wrote to Count Metternich asking him to protect the house. An official notice was pinned to the door, stating, 'This is Monet's house. Forbidden to the forces of occupation.' Blanche could stop tormenting herself.

The house may have been protected but it was nonetheless deserted. And Blanche was almost alone in knowing that the revels of Giverny had truly come to an end on that day in June 1940, when the red lorry of a travelling salesman took the last servants away.

It was done, Marguerite had handed in her apron.

THE RECIPES

A recipe from the
Café de Paris for
Florentine fillets of
sole (recipe on page 161).

Soups

Leek and Potato Soup

Soupe aux poireaux et pommes de terre

Serves 4

6 large leeks, white parts only, in 1-cm/½ inch slices
125g/4 oz unsalted butter
1 teaspoon salt
4 large new potatoes, sliced

Heat 50g/2 oz of the butter in a saucepan and lightly fry the leeks. While they are cooking, heat 1 litre/1¾ pints water with the salt to just below the boil. Add the water to the leeks, all at once. Cover the pan, reduce the heat and simmer for 45 minutes. Add the slices of potato, cover, and continue to cook for 20 minutes. Add the rest of the butter before serving.

Cream of Sorrel Soup

Potage Germiny

Serves 4

50 g/2 oz unsalted butter
2 large bunches (about 450 g/1 lb) sorrel, trimmed
1.1 litres/2 pints Clear Stock (recipe on page 112)
2 egg yolks, beaten
4 slices French bread, about 1 cm/½ inch thick

Melt 15 g/½ oz of the butter in a saucepan over low heat. Add the sorrel and stir until it wilts. Press the sorrel through a sieve, reserving the liquid.

Heat the Clear Stock with the sorrel liquid in a covered saucepan over low heat. When it is just below boiling point, remove and reserve 250 ml/8 fl oz of the stock; leave it to cool for a few minutes. Stir the beaten egg yolks into the reserved liquid. Pour this back into the saucepan, stirring constantly, and continue cooking until it starts to thicken. Do not let it boil or it will curdle.

Opposite: Soup was served at every
evening meal in Monet's house.
This is garlic soup (recipe on page 113).

When it thickens remove it from the heat but keep it warm.

Melt the rest of the butter in a frying-pan and lightly fry the slices of French bread on both sides until golden-brown.

Place one piece of fried French bread in each warmed, shallow soup bowl. Reheat the sorrel soup, stirring constantly, and when it is piping hot, pour it over the slices of bread in the bowls.

Mixed Vegetable Soup

Potage fontange

Serves 4

450 g/1 lb dried green or yellow split peas
75 g/3 oz unsalted butter, softened
1 onion, thinly sliced
2 leeks, white parts only, sliced
225 g/8 oz sorrel, trimmed and chopped
1 iceberg lettuce, trimmed and chopped
3 sprigs chervil, finely chopped
2 medium-sized potatoes, peeled and cut in half
1.5 litres/2¾ pints Rich Stock (recipe on page 113) or water
½ teaspoon salt
½ teaspoon pepper
2 egg yolks
250 ml/8 fl oz double cream or crème fraîche
8 slices thinly-sliced bread

Soak the peas in water for 2 hours then drain. Melt 50 g/2 oz of the butter in a stockpot. Add the onion, leeks, sorrel, lettuce and chervil. Cook over low heat, stirring with a wooden spoon, until the vegetables are well-coated with butter; do not let them brown. Add the soaked dried peas and potatoes, then the Rich Stock or water. Season with the salt and pepper and bring to the boil. Cover and simmer over very low heat for at least 2 hours. Strain and reheat stirring constantly.

Beat the rest of the butter into a smooth cream, then beat in the egg yolks and cream or crème fraîche. Pour this mixture into a soup tureen and pour the boiling hot soup over it. Serve with the thinly sliced bread.

Cream of Turnip Soup

Potage à la Dauphine

Serves 4

8 small, young turnips (about 550g/1¼ lb)
50 g/2 oz unsalted butter
500 ml/16 fl oz single cream or 75g/3 oz unsalted butter
Salt and pepper

Scrape and wash the turnips well and put them in a pot with 1.5 litres/2¾ pints water and the 50g/2 oz of butter. Bring to the boil, then cover and simmer on low heat for about 30 minutes or until the turnips can be crushed easily with a fork.

Remove the pot from the heat, and strain the contents, reserving the liquid. Purée the turnips. Return the turnips and reserved liquid to the pot and put the pot back on the heat. While the liquid is reheating, add the cream or the extra butter, cut into small pieces. Stir until the mixture is smooth and the butter, if used, has melted; do not let it boil. Season to taste. Serve hot.

Herb Soup

Soupe aux herbes

Serves 6

225 g/8 oz sorrel, finely chopped
225 g/8 oz fresh chervil, finely chopped
1 small iceberg lettuce, finely chopped
50g/2 oz unsalted butter
1 teaspoon coarse salt
pinch of black pepper
50g/2 oz rice

Melt half the butter in a casserole and add the herbs and lettuce, salt and pepper. Cook for five minutes, then add 1.5 litres/2¾ pints hot water and partially cover. Simmer for 15 minutes. Rinse the rice and add it to the pot. Stir it well into the greens and cook over low heat for 30 minutes. Stir the soup well, then cut the rest of the butter into small pieces and add them to the soup before serving.

To Make A Good Clear Soup or Stock

Pour faire un bon consommé

Makes 4 litres/7 pints

Carcasses and giblets of 2 boiling fowl
6 carrots
4 small turnips
2 large leeks, trimmed and split lengthways
1 celery stalk
1 large onion
2 cloves
1 sprig thyme
1 bay leaf
2 sprigs parsley
2 egg whites, beaten

Pour 5 litres/8 ¾ pints cold water into a stockpot. Add the carcasses and giblets and bring to the boil over moderate heat. Skim the surface until it is clear.

Tie the cloves, thyme, bay leaf and parsley together in a piece of muslin, to make a bouquet garni. Add the carrots, turnips, leeks, celery and onion and the bouquet garni. Cover and simmer for 3 hours, skimming from time to time. Strain.

If you want a very clear stock you must clarify it. Leave it to cool completely, then degrease it by passing absorbent kitchen paper over the surface. Return the stock to the heat and when it is hot but not yet boiling, add the beaten egg whites.

Stir very slowly until the liquid boils, then strain it through muslin.

To Make A Rich Stock

Pour faire un bouillon gras

Makes 2.5 litres/4¼ pints

1 kg/2¼ lb skirt, chuck or other cheap cuts of beef
1 beef marrow bone
3 medium-sized carrots
2 small turnips or 1 large turnip
1 onion
1 large leek, trimmed
2 sprigs parsley
1 sprig thyme
3 celery leaves
2 cloves

Pour 3 litres/5¼ pints cold water into a stockpot. Add the pieces of beef and the bone and bring to the boil, uncovered. Boil, partially covered, for 1 hour over medium heat, skimming occasionally. Tie the parsley, thyme, celery leaves and cloves together in a piece of muslin to make a bouquet garni. Add the vegetables and the bouquet garni to the pot and bring the liquid back to the boil. Reduce the heat and simmer, covered, for three hours. Strain the liquid. For a lighter, clearer stock, strain the liquid through muslin.

Garlic Soup

Soupe à l'ail

Serves 6

12 garlic cloves, peeled
salt and pepper
6 eggs
75 g/3 oz unsalted butter
125 g/4 oz croutons
150 g/5 oz parsley, finely chopped

Put the garlic cloves into a pot and add 1.5 litres/2¾ pints water. Bring to the boil and cook until the garlic is soft, about 15 minutes. Remove the garlic cloves and crush them to a smooth paste. Return this to the liquid, remove the pot from the heat and let it cool slightly.

Melt all but 50 g/2 oz of the butter and fry the croutons, turning them constantly until they are evenly browned. Put them into a warmed soup-tureen.

Break the eggs into a mixing bowl. Add 250 ml/8 fl oz of the garlic liquid, beating well to prevent curdling.

Pour the egg mixture back into the pot, stirring constantly. Add the rest of the butter. Reheat the liquid but do not let it boil or it will curdle. Pour the hot soup over the croutons. Sprinkle with the chopped parsley and serve.

Cabbage Soup with Cheese

Garbure

This dish was made on the day the pot-au-feu stew was served. The cabbage can be replaced with a purée of vegetables from the stew, or other vegetables can be used. It is to be served as an accompaniment to a consommé or stock.

Serves 6

1 green cabbage
6–8 slices day-old bread
450 g/1 lb Cheddar or Cantal cheese, grated
1 litre/1¾ pints stock

Trim the cabbage and pull the leaves apart. Blanch it in rapidly boiling water for 10 minutes, then drain it. Have another pot of boiling water ready and add the cabbage leaves to it. Cook them, covered, on low heat for 15 minutes. Drain and shred the leaves.

Preheat the oven to 200°C/400°F/mark 6. Butter an earthenware baking dish about 8 cm/3 inches deep and arrange the slices of bread to cover the bottom. Arrange a layer of cabbage over the bread, then sprinkle with grated cheese. Cover the cheese with another layer of cabbage, then another layer of cheese. Continue layering until all the cabbage is used, ending with a layer of grated cheese.

Pour the stock over the mixture. Bake about 15 minutes or until the cheese is melted and golden. Serve directly from the baking dish, pouring soup or extra stock over each serving.

Eggs

Savoury Egg Custard with Tomato Sauce

Oeufs renversés à la tomate

Serves 8

1 litre/1¾ pints milk

¼ teaspoon salt

8 eggs

100 g/3½ oz Gruyère cheese, grated

½ teaspoon pepper

Fresh tomato sauce

12 ripe tomatoes, skinned and quartered

2 sprigs thyme

1 bay leaf

½ teaspoon pepper

½ teaspoon salt

1 small slice ham, cut into julienne strips (optional)

25 g/1 oz unsalted butter, cut into pieces

Heat the milk with the salt. When it comes to the boil, remove it from the heat but keep it warm.

Preheat the oven to 150°C/300°F/mark 2. Butter a large straight-sided mould, such as a Charlotte mould. Beat the eggs, as for an omelette. Continue beating while adding the warm milk, one tablespoon at a time, until the eggs are warmed, after about 6 tablespoons. Then add the remaining milk, and the cheese. Stir and pour the mixture into the mould. Place it in a baking dish filled with enough water to come halfway up the sides of the mould. Bake for at least 30 minutes, or until the tip of a knife inserted into the centre comes out clean. Remove from the oven and leave to cool for at least 5 minutes before turning out on to a warmed serving dish.

While the custard is cooking, make the tomato sauce. Press them lightly to extract excess juice and the seeds. Put the tomato pulp into a saucepan. Cook over medium heat, stirring, and add the thyme and bay leaf. Bring to the boil and add the salt and pepper. Reduce the heat and

Opposite: Scrambled eggs with truffles were traditionally served at Christmas (recipe for scrambled eggs on page 116).

simmer for at least 20 minutes or until it turns into a thick purée. Strain the liquid and add the ham, if used. Keep warm in a bain-marie until the eggs are ready. Just before serving, remove the sauce from the bain-marie and stir in the butter, a piece at a time, until the mixture is smooth. Pour the sauce over the egg custard.

Poached Eggs au Gratin

Oeufs pochés à la lyonnaise

Serves 8

125 ml/4 fl oz vinegar

8 eggs

12 small white onions, finely chopped

15 g/½ oz unsalted butter

2 tablespoons plain flour

250ml/8 fl oz milk

250ml/8 fl oz Clear Stock (recipe on page 112)

½ teaspoon salt

½ teaspoon pepper

2 tablespoons grated Gruyère cheese

Pour 500 ml/16 fl oz boiling water into a large frying pan and add the vinegar. Break each egg individually and slide it into the boiling liquid, to poach it. Cover the skillet and cook for about 6 minutes or until all the eggs are poached. Remove each with a spatula and drain them on absorbent kitchen paper.

Put the onions into a saucepan with 125ml/4 fl oz boiling water and bring to the boil. Cook for 5 minutes, uncovered, or until slightly softened. Melt the butter in a saucepan and add the onions. Cook them gently for 5 to 10 minutes, or until they are just beginning to colour. Stir in the flour, milk, and Clear Stock; cook, stirring constantly, until you have a thick white sauce. Season with the salt and pepper.

Preheat the grill. Butter a large, shallow ovenproof dish and pour half the sauce into it. Arrange the poached eggs on the sauce and pour the rest of the sauce over them. Sprinkle with the grated cheese. Place the dish under the grill and cook under very high heat until the cheese browns and bubbles.

Stuffed Eggs

Oeufs berrichons

Serves 4

4 hard-boiled eggs
2-3 sprigs parsley, chopped
1 small onion, finely chopped
1 garlic clove, finely chopped
¼ teaspoon salt
¼ teaspoon pepper
3 tablespoons double cream or crème fraîche

Slice the eggs in half lengthways and remove the yolks. Mash the yolks and combine them with the parsley, onion, garlic, salt and pepper. Stir in the cream or crème fraîche. Fill the whites with the mixture.

Preheat the oven to 150°C/300°F/mark 2. Lightly butter a baking dish. Arrange the eggs in the dish. Bake the mixture for about 20 minutes or until the tops are lightly browned.

Eggs Orsini

Oeufs Orsini

This very easy dish is always successful, but it cannot be kept waiting when ready.

Serves 6

6 eggs
¼ teaspoon salt
¼ teaspoon pepper
2 tablespoons grated Cheddar or Gruyère cheese
50 g/2 oz unsalted butter , cut into small pieces

Break six eggs separately, pouring the whites into a bowl but leaving the yolks in their shells. Try to remove the threads from the yolks, but do not break the yolks. Prop the shells up with kitchen paper or a cloth to keep the yolks from spilling out.

Add the salt to the whites and beat them into stiff peaks. They should be capable of supporting the weight of a teaspoon without it sinking in.

Preheat the oven to 150°C/300°F/mark 2. Butter an ovenproof dish and pour the whites into it all at once. Smooth the surface with a wooden spoon. Use the spoon handle to make six fairly deep evenly-spaced cavities in the whites, as far apart as possible. Slip one egg yolk into each cavity and sprinkle them with the pepper. Sprinkle the whole dish with the cheese and dot it with the butter.

Place the dish on the floor of the oven. Bake for 30 minutes or until the yolks are set. Serve immediately.

Scrambled Eggs

Oeufs brouillés

Monet was fond of scrambled eggs with wild mushrooms, and at Christmas truffles were added to the eggs.

Serves 4

125 g/4 oz croutons
100 g/3½ oz chanterelle mushrooms (optional)
8 eggs
½ teaspoon salt
½ teaspoon pepper
125 g/4 oz unsalted butter, cut into small cubes
2 tablespoons finely chopped chives (optional)
2 tablespoons finely chopped truffles (optional)
Butter, for frying (optional)

Divide the croutons between four warmed plates. Fry the mushrooms, if using, in butter for five minutes. Heat some water in a bain-marie or double boiler. Break the eggs into a bowl, and carefully remove the threads of the whites without mixing the eggs too much. Add the salt and beat lightly, as for an omelette. The mixture must not foam. Pour the eggs into a saucepan placed in the bain-marie or double boiler. Beat them thoroughly for 2 minutes, then add the pepper and continue beating until the mixture begins to thicken. Now add the cubes of butter, one at a time, beating constantly. When the eggs are on the point of setting, add the chives, truffles or chanterelle mushrooms, if desired, and pour the mixture over the croutons on the plates.

Opposite: Monet was very fond
of wild mushrooms, which were
often added to scrambled eggs.

Sauces

Tomato Sauce

Sauce à la tomate

Makes 375ml/12 fl oz

125 g/4 oz unsalted butter
2 tablespoons plain flour
500 ml/16 fl oz boiling milk
¼ teaspoon salt
¼ teaspoon pepper
2 tablespoons tomato purée

Place the butter and flour in a saucepan and stir them into a smooth paste over low heat. Remove from the heat and gradually add the milk, stirring constantly to prevent lumps from forming. Season with salt and pepper. Return the pan to the heat and continue to cook over low heat, stirring constantly, until the liquid boils. Stir in the tomato purée, and serve hot.

Béarnaise Sauce

Sauce béarnaise

Makes 250 ml/8 fl oz

1 sprig thyme
2 sprigs parsley
2 sprigs tarragon
2 sprigs chervil
125 ml/4 fl oz white vinegar (acetic acid)
2 shallots, finely chopped
3 egg yolks
125 g/4 oz unsalted butter, softened
¼ teaspoon salt
¼ teaspoon pepper

Tie the thyme, parsley and 1 sprig each of the tarragon and chervil into a piece of muslin, to make a bouquet garni. Finely chop the remaining sprigs of tarragon and chervil. Pour the vinegar into a small saucepan. Add the shallots and bouquet garni. Bring the liquid to the boil, then reduce the liquid slowly over a low heat for about 30 minutes or until it has a syrupy consistency. Remove the pan from the heat. When the sauce has cooled to lukewarm, discard the bouquet garni. Gradually incorporate the egg yolks and butter, beating

until the mixture is smooth. Season with the salt and pepper. To finish the sauce, stir in the chopped herbs.

Tartar Sauce

Sauce tartare

This sauce is eaten as an accompaniment to every type of fish, as well as charcuterie and cold chicken.

Makes 250 ml/8 fl oz

3 hard-boiled egg yolks
2 tablespoons Dijon mustard
1 tablespoon white vinegar (acetic acid)
3 shallots
2 sprigs parsley or chervil, finely chopped
6 spring onions or 2 sprigs tarragon, finely chopped
4 tablespoons groundnut oil
¼ teaspoon salt
¼ teaspoon pepper
1 tablespoon capers

Mash the hard-boiled egg yolks with the mustard, vinegar, shallots and herbs. Add the groundnut oil drop by drop, beating after each addition, as if you were making mayonnaise. Season with salt and pepper and stir in the capers.

Hollandaise Sauce

Sauce hollandaise

Makes 250 ml/8 fl oz

225 g/8 oz unsalted butter, cut into small pieces
2 egg yolks
½ teaspoon salt
1 tablespoon wine vinegar or lemon juice
5 tablespoons whipped cream (optional)

Melt the butter with the egg yolks, salt and vinegar or lemon juice over very low heat, stirring constantly until the butter has melted. Continue stirring gently over low heat until the sauce thickens; do not let it boil. If you cannot get the heat low enough, make the sauce in a bain-marie or double-boiler. For a richer sauce, beat in whipped cream just before serving.

Horseradish Sauce

Sauce raifort, dite Radimsky

Makes 250 ml/8 fl oz

5 hard-boiled eggs
125 g/4 oz finely chopped horseradish
3 small onions, finely chopped
2 tablespoons finely chopped chives
4 tablespoons chopped parsley
1 tablespoon finely chopped chervil
¼ teaspoon salt
¼ teaspoon pepper
1 tablespoon capers
4 tablespoons Rich Stock (recipe on page 113)
1 tablespoon wine vinegar
2 teaspoons olive oil

Mash the egg yolks with the horseradish. Chop the egg whites finely and combine them with the horseradish mixture.

Mix the onions with the herbs, salt and pepper. Add this mixture to the egg-and-horseradish mixture and combine well. Add the capers. Stir in the Rich Stock and wine vinegar and bind with the olive oil.

Mayonnaise

Sauce mayonnaise

This mayonnaise is served with cold chicken or fish. To make a really good mayonnaise you need to stir the mixture rhythmically and have lots of patience.

Makes about 375 ml/12 fl oz

1 egg yolk
¼ teaspoon salt
¼ teaspoon pepper
About 1 teaspoon lemon juice or white wine vinegar
250 ml/8 fl oz olive oil
1 tablespoon finely chopped chervil (optional)
1 tablespoon finely chopped chives (optional)

Mayonnaise should be made two hours before it is required, so that the flavours combine well. Put the egg yolk, salt, pepper and lemon juice or vinegar into a bowl. Stir with a metal spoon. Add the oil, drop by drop, stirring well after each addition. Once the sauce has thickened, taste it and add more lemon juice or vinegar if necessary. Chervil and/or chives can be added at this stage.

Fresh Tomato Sauce

Sauce tomate

Makes 250 ml/8 fl oz

6 large, ripe tomatoes, skinned and quartered
1 sprig thyme
1 bay leaf
¼ teaspoon salt
¼ teaspoon pepper
25 g/1 oz unsalted butter
50 g/2 oz diced lean ham (optional)

Press the tomatoes lightly to remove excess juice and the seeds. Put them into a saucepan with the thyme and bay leaf. Season with the salt and pepper. Bring to the boil, and reduce the heat. Simmer uncovered until the tomatoes dissolve into a purée. Pass them through a sieve and keep the resulting sauce warm in a bain-marie. Add the unsalted butter just before serving, as well as the diced lean ham, if liked.

Pages 120-121:
Onions and shallots were finely chopped
to make the white butter sauce to
accompany the Sunday pike (recipe on page 157).

Appetisers and Side Dishes

Welsh Rarebit

Welsh Rarebit (recette anglaise)

Serves 10

10 large slices day-old bread, about 1 cm/½ inch thick
225 g/8 oz mature cheese (such as Cheddar), thinly sliced
4 tablespoons lager or light ale
1½ tablespoons French mustard
½ teaspoon pepper
100 g/4 oz unsalted butter

Trim the crusts from the slices of bread, cutting them into neat rectangles. Toast them evenly on both sides and keep them warm.

Meanwhile, in a frying-pan over low heat, cook the cheese with the lager or beer and mustard, stirring constantly to prevent boiling. Season with the pepper. Quickly butter each slice of toast and pour a tablespoon of the cheese mixture over it. Serve very hot.

Charlotte Lysès's Stuffed White Onions

Oignons blancs farcis (Charlotte Lysès)
This dish is delicious served either hot or cold.

Serves 4

4 large white onions
250 g/8 oz cooked roast pork, chicken or calves' liver
2 tablespoons chopped chives
2 tablespoons dried mixed herbs
150 g/5 oz grated Gruyère cheese
1 hard-boiled egg

Cut 1-cm//½-inch slices off the tops of the onions. Blanch the onions, by putting them into boiling water to cover and cooking for 30 minutes. Drain and cool. Scoop out the centre of each, leaving about a 1-cm/½-inch wall. Mince the meat and combine with the chives, dried mixed herbs and half the grated cheese. Mash the egg

Opposite: One of the recipes Monet adopted, Charlotte Lysès's stuffed white onions (recipe on this page).

yolk, chop the white and combine with the rest of the mixture. Stuff the onions with the mixture, mounding it slightly above the level of the onions.

Preheat the oven to 180°C/350°F/mark 4. Place the onions in a buttered roasting tin and sprinkle with the rest of the grated cheese. Bake for 30 minutes or until the cheese is lightly browned.

Baked Red Kidney Beans

Haricots rouges à l'étuvée

Serves 6

450 g/1 lb red kidney beans
1 teaspoon salt
1 or 2 medium-sized onions, cut into quarters
2 sprigs thyme
1 bay leaf
20g/ ¾ oz lard
125 g/4 oz green streaky bacon or pancetta rashers
4 thick slices smoked ham
6 chipolata sausages
250 ml/8 fl oz dry red wine

Soak the beans for 6 hours or overnight in fresh water to cover. Drain them, discarding the soaking water. Put the beans into a deep pot with a lid and add water to cover. Add the salt and onions, thyme and bay leaf. Bring the water to the boil, then boil, uncovered, for 10 minutes. Reduce the heat and cook gently for about 2 hours. The beans should swell but must not burst. When they are soft to the touch but not completely cooked through, strain them, reserving the cooking liquid. Discard the thyme and bay leaf and cover the beans to prevent them from drying out.

In a large pot with a tight-fitting lid, heat the lard. Add the bacon, ham and chipolatas and fry until golden but not browned. Add the beans, red wine and about 4 cups of the bean cooking liquid. Cover the pot with a piece of greaseproof paper larger than the diameter of the pot, then place the lid on top, to keep all the steam inside. Cook over low heat, without stirring, for about 2 hours, or until the liquid is very much reduced.

Stéphane Mallarmé's Recipe for Chanterelles

Recette de girolles (Mallarmé)

Chanterelles (*Cantharellus cibarius*) are orange-yellow, funnel-shaped fungi with veins instead of gills on the underside. They are to be found in the woods in autumn. This dish tastes just as good, perhaps even better, when reheated in a bain-marie or double boiler.

Serves 8

1 kg/2¼ lb fresh chanterelles
125 g/4 oz green streaky bacon or pork belly
75g/3 oz lard
½ teaspoon pepper
1 garlic clove, finely chopped
2 tablespoons chopped parsley

Trim the stems of the chanterelles and wipe them to remove the sand, but avoid washing them if possible. Cut the largest ones in half. Chop the streaky bacon or pork belly into small pieces. Fry the bacon in lard and sprinkle it with pepper.

Add the chanterelles and cook them on low heat for 1½ hours, or until their liquid has evaporated. Add the garlic and parsley and cook for another 5 minutes.

Poached Truffles

Truffes à la serviette

Serves 4

4 truffles
4 thin slices streaky bacon
About 500 ml/16 fl oz dry white wine
Unsalted melted butter (to serve)

Wash the truffles thoroughly, scrubbing them with a brush. Remove a very thin layer of peel. Place the streaky bacon in a deep saucepan and place the truffles on top. Add enough wine to cover. Cover the pot and cook on medium heat for 35 minutes.

Drain the truffles. Lay them inside a warmed napkin so that it covers them, and lay it on a warmed platter. Serve with melted unsalted butter.

My Recipe for Ceps

Ma recette pour les cèpes

This dish is even more delicious when it is reheated.

Serves 4

450 g/1 lb ceps
4 tablespoons olive oil
2 garlic cloves, finely chopped
4 sprigs parsley, chopped
½ teaspoon salt
½ teaspoon pepper

Wipe the ceps and peel the caps. Discard the tip of the stem and chop the stems finely with a sharp knife, leaving the caps whole. Arrange the stems in a shallow ovenproof dish and lay the caps on top of them. Sprinkle with the olive oil.

Preheat the oven to 170°C/325°F/mark 3. Bake the ceps for 20 minutes or until the oil is transparent. Combine the garlic and parsley. Remove the ceps from the oven and sprinkle the mixture over them. Season with salt and pepper. Return the ceps to the oven and bake for another 20 minutes, basting at least twice with the liquid in the dish.

Opposite: An extract from the notebooks on how to prepare chanterelles (recipe on this page).

Recettes des Girolles

Coupez les queues des champignons et partagez
les gros en deux. Laissez les tremper une
heure dans de l'eau afin que le sable se
détache, lavez les ensuite à plusieurs eaux
et laissez égoutter.

Prenez pour 1 kg de girolles, un demi quart
de lard de poitrine haché, un bon morceau
de saindoux, dans lequel vous faites revenir
le lard. Mettez y les champignons, et un
peu de poivre et peu de sel (le lard
sale presque suffisamment)

Laissez cuire environ 1 heure et demie
afin que l'eau que jettent les girolles soit
réduite complètement. Cinq minutes avant
de servir prenez une gousse d'ail hachée
menue avec du persil que vous mettez
dans les champignons

Les girolles sont aussi bonnes, presque
meilleures qu'à la première fois, réchauffées
au bain-marie

Stuffed Tomatoes

Tomates farcies

Serves 4

4 large, ripe tomatoes
1 sprig parsley
1 sprig thyme
1 bay leaf
1 sprig chervil
¼ teaspoon salt
¼ teaspoon pepper
125 g/4 oz fresh breadcrumbs
2 tablespoons vegetable oil
125g/4 oz streaky bacon
2 tablespoons chopped parsley
1 garlic clove, finely chopped
2 shallots, finely chopped
2 egg yolks
4 mushrooms, finely chopped (optional)

Cut 1-cm/½-inch slices off the bottoms of the tomatoes. Scoop out the centre of each, leaving about a 1-cm/½-inch wall. Place the pulp in a saucepan and cook it over high heat. When it has boiled for about 3 minutes, remove the pan from the heat and pass the contents through a sieve. Pour the purée thus obtained into the saucepan.

Tie the parsley, thyme, bay leaf and chervil together in a piece of muslin to make a bouquet garni and add it to the pan. Season with the salt and pepper. Cook for about 15 minutes over low heat, uncovered, to thicken the purée. Discard the bouquet garni and stir in the breadcrumbs. Cook for 3 minutes.

Heat the oil in a frying-pan. Combine the bacon, parsley, garlic and shallots, and fry the mixture in the oil, stirring occasionally, until the bacon is lightly browned. Add half the tomato and breadcrumb mixture. Mix well and stir in the egg yolks to bind it. At this stage, the mushrooms can be added, if used.

Preheat the oven to 180°C/350°F/mark 4. Stuff the tomatoes with the bacon-and-herb mixture. Place them in a buttered ovenproof dish and pour the rest of the tomato-and-breadcrumb mixture over them. Bake for 30 minutes or until the tops are lightly browned.

Baked Field Mushrooms

Gratin de champignons

Serves 4

225 g/8 oz fresh field mushrooms or cultivated mushrooms
50 g/2 oz unsalted butter
1 tablespoon chopped shallots
1 tablespoon cognac
15 g/½ oz plain flour
2 tablespoons double cream, clotted cream or crème fraîche
½ teaspoon salt
½ teaspoon pepper

Trim off the muddy tips of the mushroom stems and carefully wipe the mushrooms to remove sand, but try to avoid washing them if possible. Slice them into quarters, slicing the largest mushrooms once more.

In a saucepan of just the right size to hold all the mushrooms, melt the butter. Add the shallots. Cover the saucepan and cook for 10 minutes over medium heat. Add the cognac and cook for 2 minutes. Preheat the oven to 230°C/450°F/mark 8. Meanwhile, combine the flour and cream. Pour this over the mushrooms and continue to cook, stirring continually, for about 5 minutes more. Season with the salt and pepper and pour into a gratin dish or ovenproof dish. Bake for about 15 minutes or until lightly browned.

Potato Pie

Pâté de pommes de terre

Serves 8

225 g/8 oz shortcrust dough
6 medium-sized potatoes, peeled and thinly sliced
4 medium-sized onions, thinly sliced
125 g/4 oz chopped parsley
½ teaspoon salt
½ teaspoon pepper
3 tablespoons double cream, clotted cream or crème fraîche
1 egg, beaten

Butter a 20-cm/8-inch pie dish. Roll out half the dough and use it to cover the base and sides of the dish. Arrange the potato slices in the dish, and cover them with the onion rings and the parsley. Sprinkle with the salt and pepper and add the cream.

Roll out the rest of the dough and use it to make a lid for the pie. Arrange the pastry lid over the pie and make a hole in the centre. Roll a small piece of cardboard into a tube to make a funnel-shaped pie chimney and place it in the hole; this is essential to allow the steam to escape during cooking.

Preheat the oven to 180°C/350°F/mark 4. Brush the dough with the beaten egg and bake the pie for about 2 hours. If it browns too early, cover it with buttered greaseproof paper.

Glazed Carrots

Carottes fermières

This dish is very good served with braised meat.

Serves 4

450 g/1 lb sliced raw carrots
15 g/½ oz unsalted butter
1 tablespoon plain flour
2 sprigs chervil, finely chopped
4 sprigs parsley, chopped
1 sprig tarragon, finely chopped
½ teaspoon salt
½ teaspoon pepper
250 ml/8 fl oz stock
Juice of ½ lemon
1 tablespoon sifted icing sugar

Cook the carrots in 750 ml/1¼ pints boiling water for 5 minutes, or until almost cooked. Drain them, reserving the cooking liquid.

In a saucepan with a lid, melt the butter and stir the flour into it. Cook for 2 minutes, then add the finely chopped herbs, salt and pepper, 60 ml/2 fl oz of the carrot cooking liquid, and the stock. Add the lemon juice and icing sugar, and finally the carrots. Bring to the boil, then reduce the heat to very low, and place the pan half-off the heat so that it cooks very slowly. Half-cover the pan to allow the steam to escape during cooking. Cook for 1 hour, after which time the carrots should be cooked and glazed. Serve in a warmed vegetable dish.

Stuffed Aubergines

Aubergines farcies

This dish is served accompanied by Fresh Tomato Sauce (recipe on page 119).

Serves 4

4 large aubergines
1 tablespoon coarse salt
About 75 g/3 oz plain flour
250 ml/8 fl oz olive oil
225 g/8 oz chopped mushrooms
4 tablespoons chopped parsley
1 or 2 shallots, chopped
1 or 2 garlic cloves, chopped
½ teaspoon salt
½ teaspoon pepper
1 tablespoon tomato purée
50 g/2 oz unsalted butter
225 g/8 oz dry breadcrumbs

Split the aubergines lengthways. Make a few cuts in the flesh and sprinkle them with the coarse salt. Leave them for about one hour.

Rinse the aubergines, pat them dry, and coat them with the flour, dusting off the excess.

Heat the oil in a frying-pan and fry the aubergines until they are cooked through, but still firm. Drain them, reserving the oil. When they are cool, scoop out the flesh, taking care not to damage the skins. Chop the flesh coarsely.

Combine the mushrooms, parsley, shallots and garlic and season with the salt and pepper. Heat the oil again and add this mixture to the frying-pan, cooking until the mushrooms are softened. Stir in the tomato purée and the aubergine flesh.

Stuff this mixture back into the aubergine skins. Arrange the stuffed aubergines in a shallow, buttered baking dish.

In a small frying-pan, melt the butter and add the breadcrumbs, stirring until they are golden. Preheat the grill.

Sprinkle the breadcrumb mixture over the aubergines, and grill them under high heat until the breadcrumbs are just beginning to brown.

Baked Beans Provençal-style

Haricots secs à la provençale

Lentils and other pulses may be cooked in much the same way as Baked Red Kidney Beans (recipe on page 123); they are soaked overnight in water to cover.

Serves 8

1 kg/2¼ lb presoaked dried haricot beans
250 ml/8 fl oz Rich Stock (recipe on page 113)
4 tablespoons olive oil
25 g/1 oz unsalted butter
2 onions, thinly sliced
4 parsley sprigs, chopped
1 bouquet garni
1 preserved goose thigh
½ teaspoon salt
½ teaspoon pepper
¼ teaspoon nutmeg

Preheat the oven to 180°C/350°F/mark 4. Put the beans, Rich Stock, oil, butter, onions, parsley, bouquet garni and goose thigh into an earthenware pot with a tight-fitting lid. Season with salt, pepper, and nutmeg. Bake for at least 4 hours, so that the beans will be cooked and the sauce reduced and thickened.

Ceps Bordeaux-style

Cèpes à la bordelaise

Ceps (*Boletus edulis*) are also known as Penny Bun mushrooms. Found in pine woods in the autumn, they have brown caps and spongy yellow undersides with pores instead of gills.

Serves 8

1 kg/2¼ lb fresh ceps
About 500 ml/16 fl oz vegetable oil
½ teaspoon pepper
½ teaspoon salt
225 g/8 oz fine, dry breadcrumbs
2 garlic cloves, finely chopped
4 sprigs parsley, chopped

Clean the ceps well, but do not wash them. Separate the caps from the stems. Heat the oil in a large saucepan; there must be enough to cover the ceps. As soon as the oil is hot, add the ceps. Sprinkle them with pepper. Cook them for at least 1 hour, uncovered, on low heat. Drain them, reserving 2 tablespoons of oil in the pan. Sprinkle the ceps with the salt. Arrange on a heated serving dish.

While the ceps are cooking, press the dry breadcrumbs through a sieve and mix them with the garlic and parsley. Heat the reserved oil in the pan and add the breadcrumb mixture. Cook briefly, stirring, over high heat, but do not let it brown. Arrange the breadcrumb mixture in a circle around the ceps. Serve piping hot.

Stuffed Artichoke Hearts

Fonds d'artichauts farcis

Serves 6

6 artichokes
6 rashers streaky bacon
2 medium-sized onions
4 – 6 shallots
1 garlic clove
450 g/1 lb mushrooms
1 tablespoon puréed tomatoes
¼ teaspoon salt
2 tablespoons vegetable oil
125 g/4 oz unsalted butter
375 ml/12 fl oz stock
225 g/8 oz dry breadcrumbs

Trim the leaves from the artichokes. Wrap each artichoke bottom in a slice of streaky bacon and tie securely. Place in a deep pot of boiling water to cover. Cook for about 20 minutes or until the hearts are soft. Discard the bacon.

Chop the onions, shallots, garlic and mushrooms. Add the puréed tomatoes and salt. Pour the oil into a frying-pan and add half the butter. When hot, add the chopped mixture and fry for 5 minutes. Add the stock and cook, uncovered, over high heat, for about 10 minutes or until the mixture thickens. Use the mixture to stuff the artichokes. Arrange the stuffed artichokes on a buttered ovenproof dish.

In a small frying-pan, melt the rest of the butter and add the breadcrumbs, stirring until they are golden. Preheat the grill. Sprinkle the breadcrumb mixture over the artichokes. Grill them under high heat until the breadcrumbs are just beginning to brown.

Aubergine and Tomato Casserole

Aubergines aux tomates

Serves 8

12 aubergines
Coarse salt
12 medium-sized, ripe tomatoes
125g/4 oz unsalted butter
1 sprig thyme
1 clove
6 shallots, finely chopped
3 parsley sprigs, chopped
2 chervil leaves, finely chopped
1 sprig tarragon, finely chopped
1 or 2 garlic cloves, finely chopped
2 tablespoons vegetable oil
50 g/2 oz dry breadcrumbs

Slice the aubergines, but do not peel them. Sprinkle them with coarse salt and leave them for 1 hour. Peel the tomatoes, discarding the centres and seeds. Melt half the butter in a saucepan and add the tomatoes. Cook them until they are soft. Tie the thyme and clove in a piece of muslin. Put the tomatoes into a saucepan and add the thyme and clove in the muslin, shallots, parsley, chervil, tarragon, and garlic. Cook, covered, for 15 minutes. Discard the thyme and clove in the muslin.

Preheat the oven to 170°C/325°F/mark 3. Pour the oil into a deep ovenproof dish. Arrange a layer of aubergines over it, then a layer of tomatoes, then another layer of aubergines, until all the tomatoes and aubergines have been used up. Sprinkle with the dry breadcrumbs and dot with the rest of the butter. Bake for 2 hours, or until the topping is golden.

Mushroom Purée

Purée de champignons

Serves 4

50 g/2 oz unsalted butter
Juice of ½ lemon
¼ teaspoon salt
225 g/8 oz mushrooms, thinly sliced
15 g/½ oz plain flour
125 ml/4 fl oz milk

Melt half the butter in a saucepan. Add 2 tablespoons hot water, lemon juice and salt. As soon as the liquid boils, add the mushrooms. Cook them, covered, for about 10 minutes or until the juices run. Drain them, reserving the cooking liquid. Purée the mushrooms. Melt the rest of the butter in the saucepan and when it is hot, add the flour and stir well. Cook for 3 minutes, stirring, but do not let the mixture colour. Add the milk and continue stirring. When the liquid thickens, add 125 ml/4 fl oz of the mushroom cooking liquid. As soon as this boils, stir the mushroom purée into it. Stir well and serve hot.

Poultry

Stuffed Capon

Chapon farci

Morels (*Morchella esculenta*) are wild mushrooms which grow in sandy places and on burnt ground, and can be found in the spring. They are available dried from gourmet shops.

Serves 10

2 roasted onions, chopped
1 slice ham, chopped
1 chicken liver, chopped
1 chicken gizzard, chopped
50 g/2 oz sliced field mushrooms, chopped
3 morels, chopped
½ teaspoon salt
½ teaspoon pepper
4 tablespoons heavy cream or crème fraîche
125 g/4 oz unsalted butter
2 egg yolks
125 ml/4 fl oz Madeira wine
4 tablespoons dry breadcrumbs, soaked in milk and squeezed
1 capon (about 3.2 kg/7 lb), with giblets and neck
3 carrots
2 sprigs each thyme and parsley

Mix the onions, ham, chicken liver and gizzard, mushrooms and morels, salt and pepper and cream. Melt half the butter in a saucepan and add the stuffing mixture. Cook, stirring constantly, over low heat for 10 minutes or until the mushrooms are soft. Leave to cool before beating in the egg yolks and Madeira. If the stuffing is too liquid add the dry breadcrumbs.

Preheat the oven to 180°C/350°F/mark 4. Stuff the capon with the mixture, truss it tightly and place it in a roasting tin. Melt the rest of the butter and brush the skin with it. Pour enough water into the pan to come 2.5 cm/1 inch up the sides. Arrange the chicken neck, the carrots, and the thyme and parsley, tied together, around the capon. Roast for 2 hours.

Opposite: the poultry was carefully
selected, especially the Christmas
capon (recipe for stuffed capon on this page).

Chicken in White Wine Sauce

Poulet à la périgourdine

Serves 4

50 g/2 oz unsalted butter
1 roasting chicken (1.2kg/3 lb), jointed
6 shallots, 3 of them chopped
½ teaspoon salt
½ teaspoon pepper
125 ml/4 fl oz dry white wine

Melt the butter in a large, deep frying-pan and brown the chicken pieces. Remove and reserve them. Add the three chopped and three whole shallots to the pan. When they begin to brown, return the chicken and any cooking juices to the pan. Sprinkle with the salt and pepper. Reduce the heat and cook for about 45 minutes, turning the pieces from time to time. As soon as the liquid begins to dry up, add the wine. Discard the whole shallots before serving hot.

Grilled Chicken

Poulet grillé

Serves 2-4

1 small grain-fed chicken (about 1.4 kg/3 lb)
½ teaspoon salt
½ teaspoon pepper
125 g/4 oz unsalted butter, melted
4 tablespoons chopped parsley or 125 g/4 oz watercress
4 slices lemon

Preheat the oven to 200°C/400°F/mark 6. Split the chicken lengthways along the backbone, and flatten the two halves. Salt and pepper the chicken on the cavity side. Place the halves in a roasting tin, skin side up and coat them with half the melted butter. Roast for 15 minutes. Preheat the grill to maximum then remove the pan from the oven and place it under the grill. Grill for about 45 minutes, turning from time to time so that the chicken is evenly browned all over. Before serving, pour the rest of the melted butter over the chicken, and garnish with parsley or watercress and lemon slices.

Chicken Casserole

Poulet en cocotte

Serves 6

50 g/2 oz unsalted butter
4 rashers back bacon, coarsely chopped
2 onions, thinly sliced
1 roasting chicken (about 1.4 kg/3lb), trussed
250 ml/8 fl oz dry white wine
½ teaspoon salt
½ teaspoon pepper
50 g/2 oz sliced mushrooms

Preheat the oven to 170°C/325°F/mark 3. Melt the butter in a deep pot with a tight-fitting lid. Add the pieces of bacon and the onions. Fry until they are nicely browned. Remove them from the pan and replace them with the chicken. Brown the chicken all over. Return the bacon and onions to the pan and add the white wine. Season with salt and pepper. Cover the pot and seal it hermetically with a strip of pastry or a strip of muslin dipped in flour-and-water paste.

Braise the chicken in the oven for 2 hours. Remove the pot from the oven, untruss the chicken and add the mushrooms. Replace the lid and return the pot to the oven for another 20 minutes.

Fried Chicken

Poulet frit

This is a good way of using up left-over roast chicken.

Serves 4

225 g/8 oz plain flour
1 egg
1/8 teaspoon salt
4 cooked chicken quarters
2 cups vegetable oil

Combine the flour, egg, 125 ml/4 fl oz water and the salt to make a thick batter. It is essential to let it rest for at least 2 hours before use.

Dip the cooked chicken in the batter, coating it evenly. Heat the oil in a deep frying-pan. Test the heat by putting a small piece of chicken in it. If it bubbles and browns quickly, the oil is hot enough. Add the rest of the chicken pieces and brown evenly, turning frequently.

Chicken Chasseur

Poulet chasseur

The fresh tomatoes can be replaced with double the quantity of tomato purée.

Serves 4

50 g/2 oz unsalted butter
4–5 tablespoons vegetable oil
1 medium-sized, grain-fed chicken (about 1.8 kg/4 lb) jointed
225 g/8 oz mushrooms, thinly sliced lengthways
250 ml/8 fl oz dry white wine
3 tomatoes, skinned, seeded and sliced
About 1 tablespoon tomato purée
½ teaspoon salt
½ teaspoon pepper
1 sprig tarragon
250 ml/8 fl oz stock

Melt the butter with 4 tablespoons of the oil in a deep frying-pan with a lid. Fry the chicken pieces until they are lightly coloured. Reserve them. If there is not enough fat left in the pan, add another tablespoon of oil. Add the mushrooms. When they begin to give up their liquid, moisten them with the wine.

Put the tomato slices into a saucepan and cook for 10 minutes, until they are soft and the liquid is reduced. Add them to the mushrooms with the tomato purée. Season with the salt and pepper and add the tarragon. Cook, uncovered, for 10 minutes, to reduce the liquid. Add the stock and simmer, uncovered, for another 10 minutes. Return the chicken and its cooking liquid to the frying-pan. Cover and cook on medium heat for 1 hour. Arrange the chicken on a serving dish and keep it warm. If the sauce appears to be too thin, reduce it by boiling it uncovered for 10 minutes. Pour the sauce over the chicken before serving.

Braised Chicken in Red Wine

Coq au vin

This dish is excellent reheated in a bain-marie after it has been chilled in the refrigerator.

Serves 4

125 g/4 oz unsalted butter
225 g/8 oz diced back bacon
12 pearl onions
1 boiling fowl (about 2.3 kg/5 lb), cut into serving pieces
1 garlic clove
1 bouquet garni
375 g/12 oz mushrooms
4 tablespoons of brandy
500 ml/16 fl oz burgundy wine
2 tablespoons plain flour
Fried croutons (1-cm/½-inch cubes)

Melt half the butter in a flameproof casserole with a lid and fry the bacon and pearl onions until the onions are transparent. Remove and reserve the bacon and onions. Fry the chicken pieces, turning them several times as they cook. Add the garlic clove, bouquet garni, and the mushrooms (if some are rather large, slice them in half). Cover the casserole and cook for 15 minutes. Skim off the surface fat.

Add the brandy and set it alight. Add the burgundy. Cover the casserole and cook for another 35 minutes. To check whether the chicken is cooked, prick the pieces with a fork; if the juice runs clear, they are cooked, but if the juices are pink, continue cooking. When the chicken is cooked, drain it over the casserole and keep it warm.

Combine the rest of the butter with the flour to form a smooth paste. Break off bits of it, and stir them into the sauce, stirring until each has melted before adding the next. As soon as the sauce is thick and smooth, return the pieces of chicken to it. Garnish with the croutons.

Chicken in Aspic

Poulet en gelée

Serves 6

450g/1 lb leg of veal
450 g/1 lb shin of veal
2 pork rinds (about 125 g/4 oz each)
1 bouquet garni
2 carrots, sliced (optional)
2 onions, thinly sliced (optional)
2 egg whites
125 ml/4 fl oz Madeira wine
1 roasting chicken (about 1.4 kg/3 lb)
50 g/2 oz unsalted butter

On the day before, make a consommé by cooking the meat and pork rinds with the bouquet garni and the carrots and onions, if used, in water to cover. Bring to the boil and simmer, covered, for 6 hours, adding more water if necessary during the cooking. Strain and reserve this liquid. Leave it to cool, then degrease it by refrigerating it until chilled, then skimming the fat from the surface and removing any remaining fat with absorbent kitchen paper.

Reheat the liquid. Beat the egg whites into stiff peaks and add them to the liquid with the Madeira to clarify it. If the consommé does not become very clear, recommence the operation, then leave it to cool.

Preheat the oven to 180°C/350°F/mark 4. Dot the chicken with the butter, then roast for 2 hours, basting it every 15 minutes, first with 125 ml/4 fl oz of the stock and then with its own cooking liquid. Do not let it brown too much or dry out. When the chicken is cooked, remove it from the oven and leave it to cool to room temperature. Remove and discard the skin and cut the chicken into serving pieces.

Pour some of the consommé into a terrine, then add some chicken pieces. Add some more consommé and more pieces, until all the chicken pieces are in the terrine. Cover the terrine with a double layer of muslin and refrigerate it. Just before serving, arrange the pieces of chicken on a serving dish.

Chicken with Chervil

Poulet au cerfeuil

Serves 4-6

4 tablespoons vegetable oil or 50 g/2 oz lard
1 roasting chicken (1 kg/2½ lb) cut into serving pieces
1 parsley sprig
1 clove
1 bay leaf
1 sprig thyme
300 ml/½ pint dry white wine
½ teaspoon salt
½ teaspoon pepper
50 g/2 oz unsalted butter, softened
4 tablespoons plain flour
125 g/4 oz finely chopped fresh chervil

Heat the oil or lard in a large, deep frying-pan. When it begins to smoke, add the pieces of chicken and brown evenly all over. Tie the parsley, clove, bay leaf, and thyme in a piece of muslin to make a bouquet garni and add it to the pan. Add the wine and the salt and pepper, and cook over medium heat until some of the liquid has evaporated and the chicken is cooked through. Discard the bouquet garni. Remove the chicken pieces and keep them warm.

Beat the butter and flour together with the chervil. Stir the chicken sauce and, while stirring, break off pieces of the chervil butter and incorporate it into the sauce. When the chervil butter has all been incorporated, remove the sauce from the heat and pour it over the chicken. Serve very hot.

Chicken with Crayfish Butter

Poulet au beurre d'écrevisses

Serves 6

225 g/8 oz unsalted butter, softened
450 g/1 lb crayfish shells, tails and legs
500 ml/16 fl oz dry white wine
2 carrots, sliced in half
2 small onions
1 bouquet garni
½ teaspoon salt
½ teaspoon pepper
1 roasting chicken (about 1 kg/2¼ lb) trussed
1 tablespoon cornflour

To make the crayfish butter, beat the butter with 2 tablespoons hot water until you have a smooth cream. Mince the crayfish shells, tails and legs, then pass them through a sieve. Mix the purée thus obtained with the butter.

Make stock in a deep pot, by heating the wine with 500 ml/16 fl oz cold water, and add the carrots, onions, bouquet garni, salt and pepper. When the liquid boils, add the chicken and reduce the heat. Cook over medium heat for 1 hour.

Put the crayfish butter into a saucepan. Add 250 ml/8 fl oz of the cooking liquid and the cornflour, and stir until the liquid is smooth and thickened, but be careful not to let it boil.

Remove the chicken from the stock and pour the crayfish sauce over it before serving. Serve very hot.

Opposite: The recipe for chicken with crayfish butter from the cookery notebooks (recipe on this page).

ferme. Faites chauffer votre fer à gauffres,
roulez un morceau de pâte de la grosseur
que vous voudrez (selon la grandeur du
gauffrier sujet à brûler)

_____

Poulet au beurre d'écrevisses.

_____

Prenez un beau poulet blanc, faites le
cuire avec du bouillon ou de jus, un peu
de champignons, un peu de citron pour
empêcher le poulet de noircir ; prenez une
douzaine d'écrevisses, faites les cuire à l'étouffée
avec un peu de beurre, carottes et échalote ;
pilez les avec un bon morceau de beurre, faites
les revenir au beurre dans une casserole,
mouillez avec du jus du poulet, passez au
tamis ; faites fondre du beurre, mettez un
peu de farine ajoutez le jus des écrevisses,
faites les cuire toujours en remuant
la sauce et quand elle est cuite mettez
au tour du poulet

_____

Meat

Marthe Butler's Cold Beef à la Mode

Boeuf mode (Marthe Butler)

Marthe Butler's recipe is an adaptation of a classic French dish, which involves larding a boneless round beef roast with strips of bacon, marinating it in white wine and brandy, then braising it for several hours with a pig's trotter or calf's foot to make the cooking liquid jell. The meat is served cold, garnished with baby vegetables and aspic made from the strained and clarified meat cooking liquid.

Serves 4

50g/2 oz unsalted butter
4-5 rashers streaky bacon
1 kg/2¼ lb boneless sirloin
750 ml/1¼ pints meat cooking juices or stock
750 ml/1¼ pints dry white wine
5 carrots
1 onion, chopped
2 tablespoons brandy

Melt the butter in a deep pot and fry the bacon in it. When the fat begins to melt, add the roast and brown it on both sides. Remove and reserve it. Add 250 ml/8 fl oz of the meat cooking juices or stock and 250 ml/8 fl oz of the wine; add the carrots and onion. Return the meat to the liquid and cover it with a lid; cook over very low heat. While the meat is braising, gradually add the rest of the meat juices or stock and the wine. Braise for 6 hours, then add the brandy. The meat should braise for at least 7 hours. Leave to cool to room temperature before removing the meat from the pot.

Opposite: Marthe Butler's version of the classic dish, cold beef à la mode, was served on Sunday on the blue Creil china (recipe on this page).

Pages 138-139: The preparation of cold beef à la mode required some planning. The meat had to cook for seven hours. The vegetables were always ordered from Florimond the day before they were required.

Beef Pie

Pâté de boeuf

Serves 6

125 g/4 oz lean minced beef
1 onion
1 garlic clove
5 tomatoes, skinned, seeded, and coarsely chopped
50 g/2 oz chopped parsley
50 g/2 oz fresh tarragon
50 g/2 oz green streaky bacon
¼ teaspoon grated nutmeg
1 teaspoon salt
1 teaspoon pepper
50 g/2 oz unsalted butter
225 g/8 oz plain flour
50 g/2 oz lard
1 egg yolk, beaten

Mince the beef again with the onion, garlic, tomatoes, parsley, tarragon and streaky bacon. Add the grated nutmeg. Season with half the salt, and all the pepper. Melt half the butter in a frying-pan and fry the mixture, stirring frequently; it should remain moist. Pour the mixture into a dish and leave to cool to room temperature.

Make the pastry dough by combining the flour with the lard, 250 ml/8 fl oz water and the rest of the salt. Roll it into a ball, wrap it in a damp cloth and refrigerate for 20 minutes. Roll it out with a rolling-pin, then roll it in a ball again, place it in a damp cloth and refrigerate again for 20 minutes. Repeat the process once more. Then roll out half the dough to fit the bottom and sides of a 20 cm/ 8 inch greased pie dish. Fill the dish with the beef mixture, then roll out the rest of the dough to form a lid for the pie.

Preheat the oven to 190°C/375°F/mark 5. Brush the dough with the beaten egg yolk. Make a hole in the centre of the pie and roll up a small piece of cardboard to make a funnel through which the steam can escape. Insert the funnel in the hole. Bake the pie for 1 hour or until golden-brown.

Stuffed Shoulder of Lamb

Epaule de mouton farcie

Serves 8

1 shoulder of lamb, boned (about 1.8 kg/4 lb)
1 teaspoon salt
1 teaspoon pepper
50 g/2 oz lard
8 medium-sized onions, thinly sliced
450 g/1 lb partially-cooked dry haricot beans
4 potatoes, peeled and thickly sliced

Stuffing

1 rasher streaky bacon, chopped
2 tablespoons chopped parsley
2 garlic cloves, finely chopped
50 g/2 oz breadcrumbs, soaked in milk and squeezed dry
½ teaspoon salt
½ teaspoon pepper

Combine all the stuffing ingredients. Lay the shoulder out flat. Season with half the salt and pepper, then spread the stuffing over it. Roll it up, and tie it firmly with a strip of muslin. Melt the fat in a large pot with a lid, and brown the meat evenly, then surround it with the onions, beans and potatoes. Season with the rest of the salt and pepper. Add hot water to cover.

Preheat the oven to 180°C/350°F/mark 4. Cover the pot with the lid and bring to the boil on top of the stove. Transfer the pot to the oven and continue cooking the stuffed shoulder of lamb for at least 2 hours.

Grilled Steak with Mustard

Entrecôte à la briarde

Serves 1

1 fillet or small porterhouse steak (about 225 g/8 oz)
4 tablespoons Meaux mustard
25 g/1 oz unsalted butter

Spread both sides of the steak with the mustard and leave for 2 hours before grilling. Melt the butter in a frying-pan or steak pan and fry the steak on both sides.

Sacha Guitry's Shoulder of Pork

Palette de porc Sacha (Guitry)

Serves 8 to 10

1 shoulder of pork (about 2.3 kg/5 lb)
1 tablespoon coarse salt
1 teaspoon black pepper
1 bouquet garni
1 cabbage, trimmed, leaves separated
8 potatoes, peeled and cut into quarters
1 garlic-flavoured boiling sausage (about 450g/1 lb)

Put the pork into a deep pot and add water to cover. Add the salt, pepper and bouquet garni. Bring the water to the boil and when it boils add the cabbage and potatoes. Cover the pot and simmer for 2 hours. Add the sausage, and cook for another 30 minutes. Serve.

Lucien Guitry's Lamb Stew

Cassoulet de Guitry (Lucien)

Serves 8

1 kg/2¼ lb boneless lamb shoulder or mutton neck, cut into bite-sized pieces
450 g/1 lb smoked breast of goose
125 g/4 oz chopped pork fat
1 tablespoon plain flour
1 litre/1¾ pints chicken or beef stock
1 teaspoon salt
½ teaspoon pepper
1 bouquet garni
1 garlic clove, chopped
2 tablespoons tomato purée
1 large (450 g/1 lb) garlic-flavoured boiling sausage
450 g/1 lb dried haricot beans, soaked overnight
4 tablespoons chopped parsley
125 g/4 oz dry breadcrumbs

Put the meat and pork fat into a large frying-pan and fry until well browned, turning frequently. Transfer the meat to a tinned copper or flameproof casserole.

Sprinkle the meat with the flour, stir and moisten with the stock. Season with salt and pepper and add the bouquet garni, garlic, and tomato purée.

Bring 1 litre/1¾ pints water to the boil in a saucepan and poach the sausage on very low heat for 20 minutes, or until cooked through. Cut it into 5-cm/2-inch pieces and add it to the stew. Meanwhile, drain the beans, put them into fresh cold water, bring to the boil, and boil, uncovered, for 10 minutes. Add the beans to the stew, cover the pan and simmer for at least 2 hours.

Preheat the oven to 200°C/400°F/mark 6. Remove the lid from the pan, sprinkle the contents with the parsley and breadcrumbs and place in the oven. Cook for 30 minutes or until well browned on top. Serve in the pot, if possible.

Ox Tongue au Gratin

Langue de boeuf au gratin

Serves 8

1 ox tongue
2 carrots
3 onions
4 black peppercorns
1 bouquet garni
250 ml/8 fl oz dry white wine
3 pickled gherkins, sliced
3 shallots, chopped
4 tablespoons chopped parsley
140 g/4½ oz dry breadcrumbs
50 g/2 oz unsalted butter, cut into pieces

The day before, soak the tongue in cold water to cover. The next day, blanch it in boiling water to cover for 30 minutes. Remove it and drain it. Discard the bones and trim away the fat, then peel the tongue. Place it in cold water with the carrots, onions, peppercorns and the bouquet garni. Bring to the boil, cover the pot, then cook at a bare simmer for 3 hours.

Remove the tongue from the liquid. When it has cooled, slice it thinly at a slight angle. Preheat the oven to 170°C/325°F/mark 3. Butter a large, ovenproof dish. Arrange the slices on it and sprinkle them with the wine. Arrange the slices of gherkin over them. Sprinkle the dry breadcrumbs over the top and dot it with the butter. Bake for 30 minutes or until lightly-browned.

Pork Chops Foyot

Escalopes Foyot

Serves 4

125 g/4 oz unsalted butter
4 onions, thinly sliced
4 pork chops
50 g/2 oz dry breadcrumbs
50 g/2 oz grated Cheddar or Parmesan cheese
125 ml/4 fl oz dry white wine
½ teaspoon salt
½ teaspoon pepper
4 lemon wedges

Melt half the butter in a frying-pan and fry the onions until softened but not browned. Preheat the oven to 170°C/325°F/mark 3. Place the pork chops in a shallow, buttered ovenproof dish. Pile the onions on top, then sprinkle with the breadcrumbs and grated cheese. Pour the white wine into the bottom of the dish. Cut the rest of the butter into pieces and dot them over the mixture. Season. Bake the pork chops for 45 minutes or until the tops are golden. Serve garnished with the lemon wedges.

Veal with Olives

Veau aux olives

Serves 4

4 tablespoons vegetable oil
1 small boned, rolled joint of veal (about 1 kg/2¼ lb)
350g/12 oz green olives, stoned
36 pearl onions, skinned
¼ teaspoon salt
½ teaspoon pepper
1 cup hot stock or water

Heat the oil in a flameproof casserole with a lid. Add the veal and brown all over. Cover and cook on low heat for 30 minutes. Add the olives and onions. Season with the salt and pepper. Add the stock or water to the cooking liquid. Serve the cooking liquid as a sauce with the veal, and garnish with the olives and onions.

Grilled Steak with Red Wine Sauce

Entrecôte marchand de vin

Serves 1

25 g/1 oz unsalted butter
25 g/1 oz plain flour
2 tablespoons stock
4 tablespoons dry red wine
2 chopped shallots
½ teaspoon salt
½ teaspoon pepper
1 fillet or small porterhouse steak (about 225 g/8 oz)

Melt the butter in a saucepan and stir in the flour. When the mixture is smooth, add the stock. Remove from the heat. Pour the wine into another saucepan and add the shallots. Cook over high heat until the liquid is reduced by half. Strain the liquid and add it to the flour and butter mixture. Keep this sauce warm while you grill the steak on both sides. When the steak is cooked, coat it with the sauce.

Marguéry's Oxtail Stew

Queue de boeuf en hochepot (Marguéry)

Serves 6

4 pork rinds (about 225 g/8 oz)
2 sprigs thyme
1 bay leaf
1.4 kg/3 lb oxtail, cut into 6 portions
750 ml/1¼ pints beef stock
250 ml/8 fl oz dry white wine
50 g/2 oz unsalted butter
12 pearl onions
1 tablespoon icing sugar
275 g/10 oz button mushrooms
1 kg/2¼ lb chestnuts
6 chipolata sausages

Arrange the pork rinds, thyme and bay leaf in a deep pot. Lay the oxtail on top. Cook on medium heat, uncovered, for 15 minutes. Moisten with 250 ml/8 fl oz of the beef stock and cook until the liquid forms a glaze. Add the rest of the stock and the white wine. Cover the pot and cook on low heat for about 3 hours or until the flesh falls off the bone.

Meanwhile, melt half the butter and fry the onions, adding the icing sugar when they are transparent and stirring until they are glazed. In another saucepan, melt the rest of the butter and cook the mushrooms until the juices run. Cut crosses in the chestnut skins, then boil them in water to cover for 40 minutes. Peel, removing the inner and outer skins.

Transfer the oxtail to a deep frying-pan. Strain the cooking liquid and degrease it. Add the onions, mushrooms, sausages, and chestnuts. Cook for 15 minutes and serve the stew hot.

Pickled Beef

Boeuf berrichon

Serves 8

1 boned and rolled joint of beef (about 2.3 kg/5 lb)
4 rashers streaky green bacon, rinds discarded, cut into strips
2 tablespoons wine vinegar
1 tablespoon white wine
1 garlic clove
2 shallots, each stuck with 1 whole clove
1 teaspoon salt
1 teaspoon pepper
50 g/2 oz unsalted butter
About 750 ml/1¼ pints stock or water
3 carrots (optional)

Lard the beef with the strips of bacon. Place it in a deep earthenware pot with the vinegar, white wine, garlic and shallots. Season with salt and pepper. Loosely cover it with muslin and marinate for two days in the refrigerator, turning the meat twice daily.

Strain the marinade and reserve it. Melt the butter in a deep pot and fry the beef on both sides. When it is nicely browned, moisten it with about 250 ml/8 fl oz of the stock or water and 1 tablespoon of the marinade. Cover the pot and simmer on low heat for 6 hours, adding more stock or water and more marinade from time to time. The carrots should be added 1 hour before the end of the cooking time, if used.

Yorkshire Pudding

Yorkshire pudding

In France, Yorkshire pudding is also eaten as an accompaniment to roast lamb.

Serves 8

125 g/4 oz plain flour
3 eggs, beaten
500 ml/16 fl oz cold milk
½ teaspoon salt
¼ teaspoon nutmeg

Preheat the oven to 230°C/450°F/ mark 8. Butter a metal baking tin, or, ideally, grease it with fat from the roast meat. Place it in the oven.

Sift the flour into a bowl, and make a well in the centre.

Pour the beaten eggs into the well, then gradually incorporate the flour. Beat in the milk and season with the salt and nutmeg.

Pour the mixture into the heated baking tin.

Bake for about 25 minutes or until the Yorkshire pudding is well-risen and golden.

Sprinkle some meat juices over it and serve hot.

Baked Calves' Liver

Foie de veau à la moissoneuse

Serves 6

125 g/4 oz streaky bacon, coarsely chopped
125 ml/4 fl oz olive oil
4 large onions, thinly sliced
10 medium-sized potatoes
750 g/1 lb 10 oz calves' liver
½ teaspoon salt
½ teaspoon pepper
250 ml/8 fl oz dry red wine
125 ml/4 fl oz stock
25 g/1 oz butter
25 g/1 oz plain flour
2 tablespoons chopped parsley
1 garlic clove, crushed

In a large frying-pan, fry the bacon in the oil. When the fat begins to melt, remove the bacon with a skimmer and arrange it on a serving dish.

Continue to heat the oil, and when it is slightly smoking, add the onions and potatoes. Fry them over low heat, while you cut the liver into 2.5 cm/1-inch squares. Season with the salt.

Remove the onions and potatoes from the frying-pan and arrange them on the serving dish with the bacon. Add the pieces of liver to the frying-pan. Increase the heat and fry quickly, turning frequently. Drain the liver and keep it warm, covered with a cloth (a lid is unsuitable as it would retain the steam).

Discard the fat in the frying-pan and pour the wine into it. Deglaze the pan by scraping it to dislodge any bits that have stuck to the bottom and reduce the liquid by two-thirds over high heat. Add the stock and bring it back to the boil.

Combine the unsalted butter and flour into a smooth paste and break into pieces. Drop it into the sauce, stirring well after each addition. The sauce should be light. Add the onions, bacon, potatoes, chopped parsley and garlic. Cover the frying-pan and simmer for about 20 minutes.

Return the liver to the frying-pan, and cook, stirring, for 5 minutes, to reheat. Serve very hot.

Grilled Steak with Bone Marrow Sauce

Entrecôte bordelaise

Serves 1

25 g/1 oz unsalted butter
4 shallots, chopped
4 tablespoons chopped parsley
25 g/1 oz poached beef marrow
1 fillet or small porterhouse steak (about 225 g/8 oz)

Melt the butter in a saucepan and add the shallots, parsley and beef marrow. Cook until the shallots are lightly browned. Grill the steak on one side, then turn it and spread the second side with the sauce mixture. Grill that side until done. Serve hot.

Veal Cutlets, Milanese Style

Cotelettes de veau à la milanaise

Serves 4

4 veal escalopes (about 900 g/2 lb)
1 egg, beaten
½ teaspoon salt
½ teaspoon pepper
125 g/4 oz dry breadcrumbs
75 g/3 oz clarified unsalted butter
4 tomatoes, skinned, seeded and chopped
125 ml/4 fl oz meat juices
40 g/1½ oz unsalted butter
125 g/4 oz lean ham, sliced into julienne strips
50 g/2 oz sliced mushrooms
450 g/1 lb freshly-cooked macaroni or spaghetti
125 g/4 oz grated Parmesan or Gruyère cheese

Place the veal escalopes between two sheets of greaseproof paper. Beat them with a steak hammer until they are twice their original size. Pour the beaten egg into a shallow bowl, add the salt and pepper, and mix well. Pour the breadcrumbs into another shallow bowl. Heat the clarified butter in a large frying-pan. When the fat smokes, it is ready. Dip the veal escalopes in the beaten egg, then in the breadcrumbs, making sure the coating is even. Place them in the frying-pan and cook on high heat, first on one side, then on the other, then reduce the heat and allow to cook through. Remove and drain on absorbent kitchen paper.

Make a tomato sauce by cooking the tomatoes in a saucepan with the meat juices and 25g/1 oz of the butter. Do not let it boil. Add the slices of ham. Melt the remaining butter in another saucepan and add the mushrooms. Cook them until the juices run. Add the mushrooms to the tomato sauce.

Arrange the escalopes on a serving dish. Pour the sauce over the veal. Serve with the pasta, which should be ready at the same time as the veal, and hand the cheese separately. Serve hot.

Vienna Schnitzel

Escalopes de veau à la viennoise

Serves 4

4 veal escalopes (about 900 g/2 lb)
1 egg, beaten
½ teaspoon salt
½ teaspoon pepper
5 tablespoons vegetable oil
75 g/3 oz unsalted butter
125 g/4 oz dry breadcrumbs
4 hard-boiled eggs, chopped
4 tablespoons chopped parsley
4 lemon wedges

Place the veal escalopes between two sheets of greaseproof paper. Beat them with a steak hammer until they are twice their original size. Pour the beaten egg into a shallow bowl. Add the salt and pepper and a few drops of the oil. Mix well. Pour the breadcrumbs into another shallow bowl. Heat all but 15 g/½ oz of the butter along with the rest of the oil in a large frying-pan. When the fat smokes, it is ready. Dip the veal escalopes in the beaten egg, then in the breadcrumbs, making sure the coating is even. Brown evenly, first on one side, then on the other. Remove and drain.

Arrange the escalopes on a serving dish. Surround them with the hard-boiled eggs, parsley and lemon wedges. Melt the rest of the butter and sprinkle it over the veal. Serve hot.

Calves' Liver in Aspic

Foie de veau en aspic

Serves 8

1 kg/2¼ lb calves' liver
250 ml/8 fl oz Madeira or port wine
1 litre/1¾ pints stock
1 calf's foot
250 ml/8 fl oz dry white wine
1 bouquet garni
3 cloves
⅛ teaspoon mixed spice

Marinate the liver for 2 hours in the Madeira or port. Pour the stock into a casserole and add the calf's foot and dry white wine. Drain the liver and heat the marinade in a saucepan. Reduce it by half, then add it to the casserole. Add the herbs and spices, and bring to the boil. Preheat the oven to 180°C/350°F/mark 4. Place the liver in the boiling liquid. Cover the casserole and transfer it to the oven. Cook for 30 minutes. Remove the liver from the casserole and cool before serving.

Beef Rib with Olives

Côte de boeuf aux olives

Serves 4

125 g/4 oz unsalted butter
1 tablespoon vegetable oil
1 boned and rolled rib joint (about 1 kg/2½ lb)
12 pearl onions
125 g/ 4 oz streaky bacon, diced
1 bouquet garni
2 garlic cloves
½ teaspoon salt
½ teaspoon pepper
450 g/1 lb green olives, rinsed and stoned
125 g/4 oz sliced mushrooms (optional)
2 tablespoons plain flour

Preheat the oven to 180°C/350°F/mark 4. Heat half the butter in a deep pot with a tight-fitting lid. Add the oil and brown the beef on both sides. Arrange the onions and bacon around the beef. Add 500 ml/16 fl oz warm water, the bouquet garni and the garlic. Season

with the salt and pepper, then cover tightly. Bring to the boil over medium heat on top of the stove.

Transfer the pot to the oven and cook for 2 hours. Add the olives and the mushrooms, if used, and cook for another 75 minutes. Remove the meat and keep it warm in a warmed shallow bowl.

Combine the rest of the butter with the flour into a smooth paste. Cut off pieces of the paste and drop them into the cooking liquid, stirring constantly until the sauce is smooth after each addition. When the flour and butter mixture is used up, remove the sauce from the heat. Pour the sauce over the beef in the bowl.

Veal Forcemeat Balls

Boulettes de veau

Serves 4

2 tablespoons vegetable oil
2 onions, finely chopped
250 ml/8 fl oz Rich Stock (recipe on page 113)
450 g/1 lb lean minced veal
4 tablespoons chopped parsley
1 egg, beaten
1 slice bread, crusts removed, soaked in milk, squeezed dry
½ teaspoon salt
½ teaspoon pepper
¼ teaspoon grated nutmeg
50 g/2 oz plain flour
2 teaspoons lemon juice

Heat the oil and add the onions. Fry until they are transparent but do not allow them to brown. Add the Rich Stock and reduce slightly on high heat for 10 minutes. Remove from the heat and reserve.

To make the meatballs, mix the minced veal with the parsley, beaten egg and soaked bread. Season with the salt, pepper, and nutmeg. Shape into balls 2.5 cm/1 inch in diameter.

Roll the balls in the flour. Return the sauce to the heat and, when it is boiling, add the meatballs. Simmer them uncovered for 15 minutes. Add the lemon juice just before serving.

Game

Marinated Haunch of Venison

Gigot de chevreuil mariné

Serves 4

1 haunch of venison (about 1.8 kg/4 lb)
225 g/8 oz back bacon, sliced into strips
½ teaspoon salt
½ teaspoon pepper
4 tablespoons vegetable oil

Marinade

4 tablespoons vegetable oil
2 tablespoons white wine vinegar
6 carrots, sliced
6 onions, chopped
4 shallots, finely chopped
1 stalk celery, chopped
1 bouquet garni
1 bottle dry white wine

Combine the ingredients of the marinade in a large bowl. Trim the haunch and lard it with the bacon. Season it with salt and pepper. Place it in the marinade. Leave it in the refrigerator for a day or two but no longer, basting it regularly with the liquid. Strain and reserve the marinade.

Preheat the oven to 230°C/450°F/mark 8. Pat the haunch dry with absorbent kitchen paper, trim it, and brush it with the oil. Roast the haunch in a roasting tin for 1 hour, turning it several times in the course of cooking. If it looks like getting too browned, baste it with some of the reserved marinade. As soon as it is well browned all over, reduce the heat to 180°C/350°F/mark 4 and cook for another 30 minutes.

Remove the meat from the pan and deglaze the liquid, by placing it over low heat and stirring and scraping with a wooden spoon to dislodge any bits stuck to the bottom. Add 250 ml/8 fl oz of the reserved marinade and cook for 10 minutes to reduce the sauce. Serve the sauce with the meat.

Opposite: Woodcock was traditionally served for Monet's birthday (recipes on this page and on page 149).

Fried Woodcock

Bécasse à la casserole

Woodcock should be hung for several days in a cool place. It must not be drawn. When it is well-hung it can be plucked without damaging the skin.

Serves 1-2

50 g/2 oz unsalted butter
1 oven-ready woodcock
2 shallots, finely chopped
125 ml/4 fl oz dry white wine
Juice of 1 lemon

Melt the butter in a frying-pan. Add the woodcock and fry on high heat, turning frequently, for 15 minutes. Add the shallots, white wine, and lemon juice. Reduce the heat and cook for another 10 minutes.

Duck with Turnips

Canard aux navets

Serves 4

1 duckling (about 1.8 kg/4 lb) with giblets
1 teaspoon salt
½ teaspoon pepper
15 g/½ oz unsalted butter or duck fat
500 ml/16 fl oz stock
1 kg/2¼ lb turnips, parboiled for 10 minutes

Chop the duck liver and gizzard. Season them with half the salt and the pepper, and place them inside the cavity.

Heat the butter, or better still, duck fat, in a casserole with a lid. When the butter has melted or the fat is smoking, add the duck. Brown it evenly all over, turning frequently. Cover the casserole, reduce the heat, and cook for 1 hour.

Add the stock and bring it to the boil. Add the turnips; if some are larger than the others, cut them in two or four. Add the rest of the salt and bring the liquid back to the boil. Cover the pot and continue cooking on low heat for 1 hour.

Braised Pigeons

Pigeons forestière

Serves 4

125 g/4 oz lard
4 pigeons
4 carrots, sliced
125 g/4 oz mushrooms, sliced
2 onions, thinly sliced
2 stalks celery, finely chopped
½ teaspoon salt
½ teaspoon pepper
250 ml/8 fl oz meat cooking juices or stock
125 ml/4 fl oz cognac

Melt the lard in a casserole with a tight-fitting lid. Add the pigeons and fry them until they are golden-brown all over. Remove them and keep them warm. Fry the carrots, mushrooms, onions, and celery until they are soft. Mix well and remove half of them from the pot. Return the pigeons to the pot and cover them with the reserved vegetables. Season with salt and pepper, and sprinkle with the meat cooking juices or stock and cognac. Seal the casserole hermetically with a strip of pastry around the lid. Cook on low heat for about 1½ hours. Serve in the casserole.

Pigeon Stew

Pigeons en compote

Serves 4

2 pigeons
150 g/4 oz back bacon, rinds removed, diced
50 g/2 oz unsalted butter
10 pearl onions
175g/6 oz sliced mushrooms
2 tablespoons plain flour
500 ml/16 fl oz stock
500 ml/16 fl oz white Bordeaux wine
½ teaspoon salt

Trim and truss the birds. Blanch the bacon in boiling water for 5 minutes. Drain well. Melt half the butter in a flameproof casserole which is just large enough to hold the pigeons, and fry the bacon until it is well-browned. Remove the bacon, and add the onions to the pan; shake the casserole while cooking but do not touch the onions. Remove them when they are transparent and reserve them. Add the mushrooms to the pan. When they are soft, remove them and add them to the bacon and onions. Add the pigeons to the pan and fry them until they are lightly browned. Remove and reserve them.

Preheat the oven to 150°F/300°C/mark 2. Melt the rest of the butter in the casserole and stir in the flour. When the mixture is smooth, add the stock and wine. As soon as the liquid begins to boil, return the pigeons to the casserole, and arrange the onions, bacon, and mushrooms around them. Sprinkle with the salt. Cover and seal the casserole; braise in the oven for 2 hours.

Rabbit Pâté

Potine de lapin

Serves 4

6 rashers back bacon
1 rabbit, cut into 8 pieces
1 teaspoon salt
1 teaspoon pepper
1 large slice barding fat
2-3 onions, sliced into rings
1 bay leaf
1 sprig thyme
10 juniper berries
2 tablespoons brandy
500 ml/16 fl oz meat juices or Rich Stock (recipe on page 113)

Preheat the oven to 180°C/350°F/mark 4. Arrange half the slices of lean bacon in the bottom of a casserole with a lid. Arrange the pieces of rabbit on top, seasoning each piece with salt and pepper. Slice the rest of the bacon into thin strips and cover with the slice of barding fat. Add the onions, bay leaf, thyme and juniper berries. Sprinkle with the brandy.

Cover the casserole; seal it with a piece of muslin dipped in flour-and-water paste if the lid does not fit tightly. Bake for 1¾ hours. Remove from the oven and add the meat juices or Rich Stock.

Degrease it while still hot. To do this, turn out the meat on to a perforated board, retaining the juices that drain off. Leave this liquid to cool then lift off the surface grease with absorbent kitchen paper. Return the liquid to the pot, discarding the barding fat and bay leaf, and adding the meat. Refrigerate, and serve cold.

Duck in Claret Sauce

Canard à la rouennaise

Serves 4

1 duckling (about 1.8 kg/4 lb) with giblets
1 thick rasher streaky bacon
4-6 onions
1 teaspoon salt
1 teaspoon pepper
¼ teaspoon mixed spice
4 shallots, finely chopped
500 ml/16 fl oz claret
25 g/1 oz unsalted butter

The duck should be smothered to kill it, so that it loses none of its blood. Preheat the oven to 230°C/450°F/mark 8. Draw the bird and mince the liver with the bacon and onions. Season the mixture, and use it to stuff the bird, then truss it.

Roast the bird for about 30 minutes, depending on how plump it is. It should be lightly browned. Remove it from the oven and cut it into serving pieces, reserving the thighs and wings.

Butter an ovenproof dish and sprinkle it with the stuffing mixture and the shallots. Arrange the duck breast fillets on top of it. Crush the carcass in a mortar to extract all the blood. Mix the blood with the wine and pour it over the breast. Reduce the oven temperature to 150°C/300°F/mark 2. Roast the breast for 20 minutes, so that the sauce thickens, but do not let the meat cook too thoroughly or it will lose its delicate flavour. While the breast is cooking, melt the butter in a frying-pan and fry the thighs and wings until they are evenly browned.

Partridge with Cabbage

Perdrix aux choux

Serves 4

2 partridges, plucked, drawn, singed and trussed
125 g/4 oz lard
1 savoy cabbage, trimmed, leaves blanched for 10 minutes
1 slice barding fat
3 carrots, sliced
2 small onions, sliced
225 g/8 oz rashers back bacon, diced
1 pork boiling sausage
500 ml/16 fl oz stock
15 g/½ oz unsalted butter or lard, cut into pieces

Brown the partridges evenly all over in the lard. Place the barding fat in a deep flameproof casserole with a lid, and arrange half the cabbage leaves on top of it. Add the bacon and the sausage. Sprinkle with the stock and dot with the butter or lard. Cover the pot and seal it with a strip of muslin dipped in a flour-and-water paste. Cook on medium heat for at least 2 hours. If the cooking liquid is too thin, remove the meats and vegetables and reduce it over high heat, uncovered, for 10 minutes. Serve the partridges hot with the sauce in a sauceboat.

Roast Woodcock

Bécasse rotie

Serves 1-2

1 woodcock
1 thin slice barding fat
2 slices day-old bread, crusts removed, fried in unsalted butter
½ teaspoon salt

Woodcock is not drawn, except for the gizzard which is removed through a slit made in the neck. The eyes are discarded. Singe it to remove remaining feathers. Cover it with the barding fat, then truss the bird well. Preheat the oven to 230°C/450°F/mark 8. Place the bird on the fried bread in an oven dish. Roast for 20 minutes. Sprinkle with salt. Untruss, remove the barding fat and serve hot with the bread.

Venison with Rosehips

Chevreuil aux cynorhodons

Serves 4

1.8 kg/4 lb joint of boneless venison
About 250 ml/8 fl oz red wine vinegar
2 teaspoons coarse salt
6 peppercorns
1 slice barding fat
225 g/8 oz rosehips
About 500 ml/16 fl oz dry white wine
25 g/1 oz unsalted butter
25 g/1 oz plain flour
225 g/8 oz chopped almonds
4 cloves
1 lemon, seeded and chopped
2 teaspoons granulated sugar

Marinate the venison in the vinegar and 500 ml/16 fl oz water, then season with coarse salt and peppercorns. Leave for at least 2 hours, preferably overnight.

Preheat the oven to 180°C/350°F/mark 4. Grease a roasting tin and pour the marinade into it. Cover the venison with the barding fat, place it in the roasting tin and roast until tender. The cooking time will vary according to the age of the venison, but should be about 1 ½ hours. Baste occasionally with the marinade.

Clean the rosehips by trimming, washing and drying them. Split them in half and remove the seeds and hairs in the centre. Grind the rosehips and weigh them. Add the same weight of white wine to them. Place in a pan and cook for 35 minutes with 125 ml/4 fl oz of the venison cooking juices. Strain the sauce.

In a saucepan, melt the butter and stir in the flour. Add about 125 ml/4 fl oz of the venison cooking liquid and the strained sauce. Stir well. Add the almonds, cloves, lemon and sugar. Stir until the sauce has thickened.

To serve, either coat the venison with the sauce or hand it separately.

Duck Pie

Pâté de canard

Serves 8

1 duckling (about 1.8 kg/4 lb)
750 g/1 lb 10 oz boneless lean veal
250ml/8 fl oz dry white wine
3 tablespoons cognac
150 g/5 oz sausagemeat
75 g/3 oz cup dry breadcrumbs
1 rasher streaky bacon
225 g/8 oz shortcrust dough
125 ml/4 fl oz meat juices or Rich Stock (recipe on page 113)

Bone the duck. Cut the breast and thigh flesh into long strips. Do the same with the veal. Marinate for at least 2 hours in the wine and cognac.

Scrape the rest of the flesh from the bones, mince it, and mix it with the breadcrumbs and sausagemeat. Roll out half the dough and use it to line the bottom and sides of a deep 20-cm/8-inch pie dish. Cover it with a layer of the sausagemeat mixture. Arrange a layer of duck and veal meat over this. Continue until all are used up. Pat down and cover with the slice of fat bacon.

Preheat the oven to 200°C/400°F/mark 6. Roll out the rest of the dough and use it to cover the pie. Make a small hole in the centre and pour the meat juices through it. Bake the pie for 3 hours. Serve cold.

Opposite: The recipe for venison with rosehips (see above), carefully recorded in one of the notebooks.

Sanglier ou chevreuil à la sauce aux fruits d'églantiers.

Mettre la viande dans deux tiers d'eau et un tiers de vinaigre, poivre et sel ; et faire cuire jusqu'à ce que la viande devienne tendre.

Pour faire la sauce mettre, pour trois livres de viande un demi litre de fruits d'églantier qu'on a d'abord nettoyés, lavés et séchés ; les piler dans un mortier et les mettre ensuite dans un pot avec la même quantité de vin blanc que de fruits et faire cuire le tout pendant une demi heure en y ajoutant un peu du jus de la cuisson de la viande, puis passer au tamis. Ensuite on fait un petit roux, bien revenu, auquel on mélange ½ du jus de la cuisson de la viande et ½ la sauce faite avec les fruits.

Prendre un quart d'amandes douces râpées ; soi et un demi citron haché menu, des clous de girofle et un morceau sucre

Fish

Mussels with Fresh Herbs

Moules au vert

Serves 4

4 dozen mussels (about 1.5 litres/2¾ pints)
50 g/2 oz unsalted butter
2 onions, coarsely chopped
4 sprigs parsley
2 stalks celery
1 teaspoon coarse salt
1 teaspoon freshly-ground black pepper
125 g/4 oz chervil
450 g/1 lb sorrel
125 g/4 oz chopped parsley
2 tablespoons chopped tarragon
125 ml/4 fl oz dry white wine
125 ml/4 fl oz stock
1 tablespoon cornflour

Wash the mussels well in lots of cold water. Discard any that are not tightly closed or that are broken. Put them in a deep pot with half the butter, the onion, parsley sprigs, celery and salt and pepper. Cover and cook on high heat for about 10 minutes, shaking the pan vigorously from time to time, until the shells open. Discard any that are still closed. Put them into a colander, reserving the cooking liquid.

In a frying-pan, melt the rest of the butter, and add the chervil, sorrel, chopped parsley and tarragon. Add the cooking liquid from the mussels and the white wine. Add the stock and stir in the cornflour until the sauce is smooth. Reheat the mussels in the sauce. If liked, the mussels can be shelled before serving.

Opposite: Despite the difficulties of finding them, fish and crustaceans were often served at Alice's table. Here are mussels with fresh herbs (recipe on this page).

Marinated Fried Sole

Filets de sole à la Horly

Fillets of whiting can be substituted for sole in this recipe.

Serves 4

500 ml/16 fl oz vegetable oil
Juice of 1 lemon
4 tablespoons chopped parsley
1 onion, thinly sliced
4 fillets of sole, skinned
½ teaspoon salt
½ teaspoon pepper
125 g/4 oz plain flour

Prepare a marinade from half the oil, the lemon juice, parsley, and onion. Place the fish in the marinade, and season it with salt and pepper. Leave for 2 hours in the refrigerator.

Drain the fish and dip it in the flour. Heat the rest of the oil in a frying pan, and when it smokes, fry the fish until it is well browned.

Oyster Soup

Potage aux huîtres

Serves 6

3 dozen oysters
500 ml/16 fl oz court-bouillon (recipe on page 154) or chicken stock
250 ml/8 fl oz Madeira
4 peppercorns

Poach the oysters in their own liquid, plus 500 ml/16 fl oz water. When they are cooked, after about 10 minutes, reserve 1 oyster per person and remove the rest from the shells. Reserve the cooking liquid and chop the remaining oysters finely. Strain the cooking liquid and add it to the chopped oysters. Add the court-bouillon or chicken stock, then add the Madeira and peppercorns. Pour this mixture into a stockpot and bring to the boil. Boil, uncovered, for 10 minutes to allow the liquid to reduce slightly. To serve, place a whole oyster on the shell in each bowl before pouring the soup into it.

Sole in Shellfish Sauce

Soles à la normande

Serves 8

2 dozen oysters, shucked, liquid reserved
3 dozen small shrimps, shelled and deveined
2 dozen mussels
250 ml/8 fl oz dry white wine
2 dover or lemon soles (1 kg/2¼ lb), cleaned and gutted
2 tablespoons plain flour
75 g/3 oz unsalted butter
2 egg yolks
2 tablespoons double cream or crème fraîche
Juice of ½ lemon
½ teaspoon salt
½ teaspoon pepper
Slices of truffles poached in Madeira

Court-bouillon

4 tablespoons Calvados
500 ml/16 fl oz dry white wine
1 leek, white part only, sliced
1 carrot, split in half
1 large onion, thinly sliced
1 whole garlic clove
1 bouquet garni
1 teaspoon coarse salt
5 peppercorns

Put all the court-bouillon ingredients into a pan. Add 500 ml/16 fl oz water and bring to the boil. Cover and simmer for 30 minutes. Strain through a conical sieve. Poach the oysters in their own liquid, covered, for 5 minutes. Retain the cooking liquid and keep the oysters warm. Poach the shrimps in the court-bouillon for 10 minutes. Drain the shrimps, keeping them warm; reserve the cooking liquid. Wash the mussels well in a lot of cold water, discarding any that are broken or not tightly closed. Pour the white wine into a pan and add the mussels. Cover them tightly and cook, shaking the pan vigorously, over high heat for 5 minutes, or until they are all opened. Discard any that are still closed. Combine the cooking liquid with the liquid from the court bouillon and reserve the mussels.

Preheat the oven to 200°C/400°F/mark 6. Descale and trim the soles. Thickly butter an ovenproof dish and place the soles in it. Cover them with some of the cooking liquid and cover them with buttered grease-proof paper. Cook for 20 minutes.

Meanwhile, combine 25 g/1 oz of the butter with the flour. Pour 300 ml/½ pint of the fish cooking liquid into a saucepan and add the butter-and-flour mixture. Stir constantly until smooth. Remove from the heat and cool for 10 minutes. Beat in the egg yolks and cream and reduce the heat. Add the rest of the butter, cut into small pieces, and the lemon juice, still beating constantly. Season with salt and continue stirring until smooth.

Arrange the reserved shellfish around the soles in the ovenproof dish. Coat with the sauce and decorate with the poached truffles.

Fish Soup

Soupe aux poissons

Serves 10

2 leeks, white parts only, sliced lengthways
3 carrots, split lengthways
4 onions, quartered
1 teaspoon salt
1 teaspoon pepper
1 kg/2¼ lb mixed fish
2 egg yolks, beaten
225 g/8 oz fried croutons

Put the leeks, carrots, and onions into a stockpot and add 4 litres/7 pints water . Bring to the boil, then simmer for 1½ hours. Season with the salt and pepper and add the fish, cut into serving pieces. Cook on low heat for 20 minutes, then remove the most presentable pieces of fish and keep them warm. Remove the pot from the heat and let the liquid cool for 10 minutes. Add the beaten egg yolks, and stir well. Strain the liquid. Chop the fish which remained in the pot and add them to the strained liquid. Return the soup to the heat to warm it, but do not let it boil. Arrange the pieces of fish kept warm in the bowls and pour the soup over them. Garnish with the croutons.

Lobster American-style

Homard à l'américaine

Serves 4

1 large, uncooked lobster (about 1 kg/2 ¼ lb)
3 tablespoons vegetable oil
1 teaspoon salt
1 teaspoon pepper
175 g/6 oz unsalted butter
1 onion, finely chopped
3 shallots, finely chopped
1 garlic clove, crushed
125 ml/4 fl oz cognac
500 ml/16 fl oz dry white wine
1/8 teaspoon cayenne pepper
2 tablespoons stock

Chop the lobster into serving pieces. Remove the claws. Separate the body from the tail, retaining the liquid which runs out. Cut the body into two parts, and slice the tail into sections. Reserve the coral and the intestines. Pass them through a sieve.

Heat the oil to smoking hot in a frying-pan and sauté the lobster flesh in it. Season with half the salt and pepper. Cook for 5 minutes, then remove the lobster and discard the oil it has been cooked in.

Heat 40 g/1½ oz of the butter in the frying-pan and put the pieces of lobster back into it along with the onion, shallots and garlic.

Warm the cognac and set it alight before adding it to the pan. Add the wine, salt and pepper, and the cayenne pepper.

As soon as the liquid starts to bubble, cover the frying-pan and simmer for 20 minutes. Remove the lobster pieces and keep them warm.

Reduce the sauce over high heat, uncovered. Add the reserved liquid from the body, the coral and the intestines. Stir in 25 g/1 oz of the butter, and add the stock, stirring constantly. Remove the frying-pan from the heat and continue stirring and adding more pieces of butter, stirring well after each addition.

Pour the sauce over the warm lobster and serve the dish immediately.

Brill Dugléré-style

Barbue à la Dugléré

Serves 6

2 onions, sliced
4-6 medium-sized tomatoes, skinned, seeded and crushed
2 shallots, sliced
2 sprigs parsley
1 sprig thyme
1 bay leaf
1 large brill (about 1.8 kg/4 lb), descaled, cleaned and gutted
½ teaspoon salt
½ teaspoon pepper
250 ml/8 fl oz dry white wine
250 ml/8 fl oz fish stock
25 g/1 oz unsalted butter, cut into pieces

Preheat the oven to 200°C/400°F/mark 6. Butter a deep ovenproof dish large enough to hold the fish. Cover the bottom with the onions, tomatoes and shallots. Tie the parsley, thyme and bay leaf together to make a bouquet garni. Add it to the dish. Lay the fish on this bed. Season with salt and pepper. Moisten with the wine and fish stock.

Bring to the boil, cover the casserole with buttered greaseproof paper, and transfer it to the oven. Bake for 20 minutes, then remove the dish from the oven but do not turn the oven off.

Carefully pour the sauce into a bowl. Strain it, and pour it into a saucepan. Cook on medium heat, stirring constantly, and adding the butter a piece at a time, stirring well after each addition.

When the sauce is smooth and thick, pour it over the brill. Return the dish to the oven and reheat for 5 minutes. Serve in the dish.

Oysters with Sausages

Huîtres aux saucisses

When serving oysters, serve well-grilled, very hot cocktail sausages at the same time. The two are eaten together and complement each other very well.

Mackerel Fillets in Maître d'Hotel Sauce

Filets de maquereaux à la flamande

Serves 4

4 mackerel, carefully filleted
2 eggs, beaten
50 g/2 oz plain flour
125 g/4 oz unsalted butter

Maître d'hotel sauce

25 g/1 oz unsalted butter
25 g/1 oz plain flour
4 tablespoons chopped parsley
2 spring onions, finely chopped
½ teaspoon salt
½ teaspoon pepper
1/8 teaspoon grated nutmeg
Juice of ½ lemon

Melt the 125 g/4 oz butter in a frying-pan. Dip the mackerel in the beaten egg then dust with the flour. Fry until evenly browned. Keep warm.

Melt the 25 g/1 oz butter in a saucepan and add the flour. Cook, stirring over low heat. Add the parsley, spring onions, 125 ml/4 fl oz water, salt, pepper, and nutmeg. Stir until the sauce is smooth and thickened. Add the lemon juice at the last moment.

Lobster Newburg

Homard à la Newburg

Serves 4

2 small (450 g/1 lb) uncooked lobsters
2 litres/3½ pints court-bouillon (recipe on page 157)
125 g/4 oz butter
1 teaspoon salt
1 teaspoon pepper
250 ml/8 fl oz Madeira
500 ml/16 fl oz double cream
4 egg yolks

Heat the court-bouillon to boiling and plunge the lobsters into it. Cover the pot and simmer for about 25 minutes. Leave the lobsters to cool in the liquid. Split them open and remove the flesh. Remove the flesh from the claws.

Melt the butter in a frying-pan with a lid and add the pieces of lobster. Season with salt and pepper. Heat gently for 5 minutes on each side. Add the Madeira. Cover the frying-pan and simmer for 15 minutes. Beat the cream with the egg yolks. Beat this mixture into the liquid in the frying-pan, stirring until the sauce thickens. Stop stirring and cook for 5 minutes but do not allow to boil. Serve hot.

Monkfish American-style

Baudroie à l'américaine

If the cooked fish steaks are sprinkled with 2 tablespoons of cognac or Armagnac and set alight, the sauce will be even more delicious.

Serves 4

4 monkfish steaks (about 1kg/2¼ lb)
125 g/4 oz plain flour
250 ml/8 fl oz vegetable oil
4 shallots, finely chopped
1 bouquet garni
¼ teaspoon chilli pepper
500 ml/16 fl oz dry white wine
½ teaspoon salt
½ teaspoon pepper
2 tablespoons tomato purée
125 ml/4 fl oz Madeira
450 g/1 lb freshly cooked long-grained rice

Wipe the fish steaks and dust them with the flour. Heat the oil in a frying-pan and brown them on both sides. Drain off the oil. Add the shallots, bouquet garni, chilli pepper, and white wine to the pan. Season with the salt and pepper. Cover and simmer for 15 minutes.

Dilute the tomato purée in 250 ml/8 fl oz of the cooking liquid. Add this to the frying-pan with the Madeira. Cook for 5 minutes. Serve the fish surrounded by the rice and sprinkled with the sauce.

Salt Water Fish Stock

Eau de sel pour la cuisson des poissons

Makes 3 litres/5¼ pints

3 tablespoons coarse salt

This salt water stock, also known in French as 'bonne eau' or good water is used for poaching some types of fish. Catfish, brill and turbot are some of the fish that are cooked in this way. Pour 3 litres/5¼ pints water into a fish kettle or pan large enough to hold the fish. There should be enough water to cover the fish completely. Add the salt, and bring the water to the boil. Reduce the heat and place the fish in the liquid, which should merely tremble, not boil. Cooking time is about 20 minutes per pound depending on the exact weight of the fish.

How to Cook Prawns, Shrimps and Crabs

Cuisson des crevettes et des crabes

Salt the water with sea-salt. Add whole peppercorns, then small quantities of parsley and thyme and a bay leaf. Bring the water to the boil and plunge the crustaceans into it. Shrimps and prawns should cook from 2 to 4 minutes and crab from 5 to 15 minutes, depending on size. Serve warm.

Pike in White Butter Sauce

Brochet au beurre blanc

Serves 6-8

1 pike (about 1.8 kg/4 lbs), cleaned and gutted, scales left on

Court-bouillon

1 litre/1¾ pints dry white wine
2 onions, sliced
2 carrots, sliced
1 bouquet garni
1 teaspoon salt

White butter sauce

125 g/4 oz unsalted butter
2 shallots, finely chopped
1 teaspoon white wine vinegar
½ teaspoon salt
½ teaspoon pepper

Pour all the court-bouillon ingredients into a fish-kettle and add 2 litres/3½ pints water. Cover and simmer for 30 minutes. Remove the fish-kettle from the heat and let the contents cool to room temperature. Place the pike in the court-bouillon, cover the kettle, and bring the liquid back to the boil. Reduce the heat and leave the kettle half off the heat source, so that the water barely moves. If the liquid boils, the fish flesh will disintegrate. Cook the fish for 40 minutes, or 20-25 minutes per kg (10 minutes per pound).

When the fish is almost cooked, prepare the sauce. Melt the butter in a saucepan with the shallots, vinegar, salt, and pepper. Stir on low heat until the sauce thickens, but do not let it boil. Serve it in a warmed sauceboat. Serve the fish on a folded napkin.

Pages 158-159: A pike like this would be gently poached in a court-bouillon and served with white butter sauce (recipe on this page).

Lobster Douglas

Homard à la Douglas

Cooked mushrooms and truffles could be used to garnish this dish.

Serves 4

1 large live lobster (about 1 kg/2¼ lb)
375 g/12 oz unsalted butter
½ teaspoon salt
½ teaspoon cayenne pepper
125 ml/4 fl oz gin
2 tablespoons double cream or crème fraîche
15 g/½ oz plain flour

Court-bouillon

2 onions, each studded with 1 clove
5 peppercorns
1 large carrot
1 tablespoon coarse salt
2 sprigs thyme
1 bay leaf

Mirepoix

2 carrots, thinly sliced
2 onions, chopped
½ teaspoon dried thyme
1 bay leaf

In a large pot, combine the ingredients for the court-bouillon with 2 litres/3½ pints water and bring them to the boil. Plunge the lobster into the boiling liquid. Cover the pot and cook on reduced heat for about 25 minutes. Leave the lobster to cool in the liquid. When it is cold, carefully remove the flesh from the shell. Cut it into bite-sized pieces.

Place the shell and the coral in a mortar and mince it with 275 g/10 oz of the butter. Cook the mixture over low heat with the cold water. Bring it to the boil, and simmer on very low heat for 15 minutes. Remove the pot and leave it to cool then refrigerate it until the lobster butter rises to the surface. Skim off the butter and place it in a strainer.

Place 125 g/4 oz of the lobster butter in a deep frying-pan. Melt it and add the mirepoix mixture. Cook

on low heat for 15 minutes, or until the onions are lightly browned. Place the pieces of lobster over the mixture. Season with the salt and cayenne pepper. Turn the meat over and sprinkle it with the gin. Set it alight. Moisten with the cream, while stirring. Continue to stir until the liquid boils, then add the rest of the lobster butter. Stir and cook until the butter is incorporated. Combine the rest of the fresh butter with the flour to make a paste. Break the paste into several pieces and add them one by one to the sauce, stirring well after each addition. Pour the sauce under and over the lobster and serve.

Salt Cod Croquettes

Croquettes de morue

Serves 4

450 g/1 lb salt cod
About 1 litre/1¾ pints milk or water
5 potatoes, peeled
3 eggs, beaten
50 g/2 oz plain flour
500 ml/16 fl oz vegetable oil

Béchamel sauce

65 g/2½ oz plain flour
65 g/2½ oz unsalted butter
125 ml/ 4 fl oz hot milk

Place the salt cod in a colander, skin uppermost and soak it for 24 hours, changing the water occasionally. Place the cod in the milk or water and bring to the boil. Reduce the heat until the liquid barely moves and cover the pan. Cook for 15 minutes.

Boil the potatoes in water to cover. Drain them and mash them. Remove the cod from the pan and purée it while it is still hot. Combine the potatoes and the cod.

Make the sauce by combining the flour and butter in a saucepan. Stir until smooth, then add the milk all at once. Continue to stir until it is smooth and thick.

Stir the sauce into the cod mixture and add 2 beaten eggs. Heat the oil in a frying-pan. Shape the mixture into croquettes. Roll them in the flour, dip them in the remaining beaten egg and deep-fry until golden.

Florentine Fillets of Sole

Filets de sole à la florentine

Serves 4

1 litre/1¾ pints court-bouillon (recipe on page 154)
4 fillets of sole
225 g/8 oz spinach
250 ml/8 fl oz thick Béchamel Sauce (recipe on page 160)
50 g/2 oz grated Gruyère cheese

Pour the court-bouillon into a fish kettle and poach the sole fillets in it for 15 minutes. Remove and drain them. In a saucepan, cook the spinach in its own liquid until it wilts. Drain and squeeze to remove excess moisture.

Arrange the spinach in a buttered, ovenproof dish and lay the sole fillets on top. Preheat the oven to 230°C/450°/mark 8. Pour the sauce over the fish and sprinkle with the grated cheese. Bake for 10 minutes, or until the cheese melts and bubbles. Serve very hot, or the sauce will separate.

Fish Creole

Poisson à la créole

Other white fish can be substituted for the cod.

Serves 6

6 cod steaks (about 1.8 kg/4 lb)
3 teaspoons salt
½ teaspoon pepper
Juice of 1 lemon
125 g/4 oz unsalted butter
1 hot red chilli pepper, seeded and chopped
1 bouquet garni
450 g/1 lb long-grained rice
2 tablespoons tomato purée
1 egg yolk

Soak the cod in water to cover with 1 teaspoon of the salt and the lemon juice for 2 hours. Drain and pat dry. Melt half the butter in a frying-pan and add the cod steaks; add enough hot water to cover . Then add the chilli pepper and the bouquet garni. Season with 1

teaspoon of the salt and the pepper. Cover the pan and simmer for 15 minutes. Remove the fish and reserve it.

Rinse the rice and sprinkle it into a deep pot containing 2.3 litres/4 pints boiling water and the rest of the salt. Stir, cover tightly and bring to the boil. Reduce the heat and cook for 15 to 20 minutes.

Dilute the tomato purée with some of the fish cooking liquid. Add to the contents of the frying-pan and stir to incorporate. Boil uncovered for 20 minutes, or until the liquid is reduced. Bind with the egg yolk as soon as the rice is ready. Do not let the sauce boil.

Preheat the oven to 200°C/400°F/mark 6. Pour the rice into a colander and rinse it under cold water, then drain it again. Pile it into a large dish and leave it in the oven, stirring the grains from time to time to keep them separate. Place the fish in the centre of the dish with the rice surrounding it. Pour the sauce over the fish.

Mixed Fish Stew

Costriade

Serves 6

25 g/1 oz unsalted butter
2 onions, chopped
½ teaspoon salt
½ teaspoon pepper
1 bouquet garni
2 garlic cloves
450 g/1 lb potatoes, peeled and cut into large pieces
1 kg/2¼ lb mixed fish (hake, mackerel, sardines, conger eel, shrimps, crabs, mussels, etc.)

In a large deep pot, melt the butter and sauté the onions. When they are lightly browned, add 2 litres/3½ pints water. Season with salt and pepper. Add the bouquet garni, garlic and potatoes. Bring the water to the boil and boil, covered, for 20 minutes.

Slice the larger fish into pieces, leaving the sardines and crustaceans whole. Add them to the pot. Reduce the heat and inspect the pot occasionally to make sure the fish do not disintegrate.

Serve the fish and potatoes in a shallow bowl, and pour the stock over slices of bread.

Sole Fillets in Véron Sauce

Filets de sole à la Véron

Serves 8

8 fillets of sole
75g/3 oz unsalted butter, melted
4 tablespoons plain flour

Véron sauce

2 egg yolks, beaten
250 ml/8 fl oz reduced fish stock
50 g/2 oz unsalted butter
1 tablespoon double cream or crème fraîche
250 ml/8 fl oz dry white wine
250 ml/8 fl oz white wine vinegar
1 teaspoon chopped tarragon
1 teaspoon chopped chervil
1 teaspoon chopped shallots
½ teaspoon salt
250 ml/8 fl oz vegetable oil
1 tablespoon meat glaze
¼ teaspoon cayenne pepper

To make the sauce, beat the egg yolks into the reduced fish stock. Beat in the butter and cream; reserve.

Pour the white wine into a small saucepan. Add the vinegar and chopped herbs, and season with the salt. Boil until it is reduced by half, then leave to cool. Strain the sauce and return it to the saucepan. Cook over low heat beating with a wire whisk, while gradually adding the oil, beating constantly as for mayonnaise. When the oil is fully incorporated, beat in the meat glaze, and the reserved fish stock. Sprinkle with the cayenne pepper.

Preheat the grill. Dip the fillets of sole in the melted butter, then in the flour. Grill them under a low heat. When they are lightly-browned on both sides, arrange them on a napkin and serve with the sauce.

Cézanne's Salt Cod Soup

Bouillabaisse de morue (Cézanne)

Serves 6

1 large piece of salt cod (about 450 g/1 lb)
500 ml/16 fl oz olive oil
50 g/2 oz plain flour
6 potatoes, sliced
4 leeks, white parts only, sliced
½ teaspoon pepper
¼ teaspoon ground cloves
2 garlic cloves, finely chopped
2 tablespoons chopped parsley
1/8 teaspoon saffron
1 bay leaf

Place the salt cod in a colander, skin uppermost and soak it in water for 24 hours to remove the salt, changing the water occasionally. Drain well and pat dry.

Heat the oil in a frying-pan. When it is smoking, dust the salt cod with flour and place it in the frying-pan. Fry it until it is cooked through; it will not brown. Remove it, drain it and reserve it. Fry the potatoes in the same frying-pan for about 10 minutes or until they are almost cooked through.

Pour 2 tablespoons of the olive oil used for frying into a deep, cast-iron pot. Add the leeks and fry them on low heat. Remove them from the pot and reserve them. Slowly add the pepper, cloves, garlic, parsley, saffron, bay leaf, and the rest of the flour, which will brown in the oil. Add 1.5 litres/2¾ pints hot water and boil, covered, on high heat for 10 to 15 minutes. Slide the cod and potatoes into the pot, and add the leeks.

Opposite: Recipe from the cookery notebooks for shoulder of pork contributed by Sacha Guitry (recipe on page 140) and for Cézanne's salt cod soup (recipe on this page).

Palette de porc (sacha)

—

mettre la palette à cuire dans de
l'eau froide quand elle bout on
met les choses, les pommes de terre
laisser cuire 2 heures; ajouter le
saucisson — laisser cuire ½ heure
et servez —

—

Bouillabaisse de Morue (éjeune)

faire tremper la morue pour
la dessaler — La faire pocher ne
pas attendre qu'elle soit croustillante
faire frire à 3/4 de la cuisson des
pommes de terre coupées en tranches,
Mettre dans une casserole de l'huile
dans laquelle on fait revenir des
tranches, fines de poireaux pendant
ce temps assaisonner de poivre clous
de girofle et persil haché, safran
1 feuille de laurier et faire brunir une
peu de farine le tout doit être
fait très lestement — Mettre l'eau
chaude 1 verre par personne après

Desserts

Green Cake

Vert-vert

Serves 8-10

Cake

4 eggs
175 g/6 oz granulated sugar
125 g/4 oz plain flour, sifted
50 g/2 oz ground pistachios
4 tablespoons kirsch
25 g/1 oz unsalted butter, softened
Grated rind of 1 lemon

Pistachio buttercream

4 tablespoons ground pistachio nuts
2 tablespoons kirsch
500 g/18 oz unsalted butter, softened
2 teaspoons spinach colouring (see below)
75 g/3 oz granulated sugar
2 eggs
2 yolks
2 teaspoons plain flour
250 ml/8 fl oz milk

Fondant icing

725 g/1½ lb granulated sugar
1 tablespoon liquid glucose
1 teaspoon spinach colouring (see below)
Juice of 1 lemon

Spinach colouring

275 g/10 oz spinach

First make the spinach colouring. Bring 125 ml/4 fl oz water to the boil and blanch the spinach in it for 1 minute. Strain the liquid and sieve the spinach. This will produce a green purée to colour the pistachio buttercream and the icing.

Preheat the oven to 150°C/300°F/mark 2. Butter a 20-cm/8-inch cake tin. To make the cake, place a saucepan on a low heat and break the eggs into it. Beat them with the sugar until the mixture has doubled in volume. Beat in the flour until it is completely incorporated. Add the pistachio nuts, kirsch, softened butter and lemon rind. Stir well with a wooden spoon or spatula. Turn the mixture into the cake tin and bake for 30 minutes. Test with a knife to see if the cake is done. If so, remove it from the oven, turn it upside down on a wire rack and leave it to cool.

To make the fondant icing, dissolve the sugar in a heavy pan with 500 ml/16 fl oz water. Cook, without stirring, on high heat until the sugar dissolves and begins to boil. Check the cooking stage during the boiling. When the syrup reaches the large thread stage (that is, when a little of the syrup is dropped in cold water it forms a large thread), add the liquid glucose and the spinach colouring, and remove from the heat.

Lightly oil a marble work surface. Pour the syrup on to the surface and work it with a wooden spatula, until it starts to become opaque. Sprinkle with the lemon juice and continue working until it is a pale green smooth paste. Roll it into a ball and wrap it in a damp cloth. Refrigerate it until required.

To make the buttercream, combine the pistachio nuts, kirsch and 25 g/1 oz of the softened butter into a smooth paste. Colour it with the spinach colouring. In a saucepan off the heat, combine the sugar with the whole eggs and the yolks. Beat in the flour and milk, stirring constantly. Heat this mixture over a low heat, stirring, and beat in the pistachio paste. Remove the mixture from the heat and beat in the rest of the softened butter.

Carefully slice the cake into three equal layers. Spread two of the layers with the pistachio cream, then reconstitute the cake. Refrigerate it for 1 hour for the buttercream to set. Roll out the fondant icing with a rolling pin and use it to cover the cake.

Opposite: One of Marguerite's specialities
was the beautiful green cake called
the *vert-vert* (recipe on this page).

Christmas Pudding (a good one)

Christmas pudding (de bonne)

Serves 12

450 g/1 lb suet, chopped
225 g/8 oz plain flour
12 eggs
165 g/5½ oz seedless raisins
165 g/5½ oz currants
75 g/3 oz icing sugar
Rind of 1 lemon, finely chopped
175ml/6 fl oz brandy
250 ml/8 fl oz milk
125 g/4 oz dry breadcrumbs

Put the fat and flour into a bowl. Break the eggs into it and add the raisins and currants, as well as the sugar, chopped lemon peel, and half the brandy. Mix well with a wooden spoon. Add the milk and breadcrumbs, to make a mixture that is light and smooth, though stiff.

Fill a large pot with enough water to cover the pudding and bring it to the boil. Butter and flour a pudding cloth. Place the mixture in it and shape it into a ball. Tie the four corners of the cloth tightly together, leaving room inside for the pudding to expand. Put the pudding into the pot and half-cover it. Boil the pudding on low heat for 5 to 6 hours, adding boiling water from time to time to ensure that the level does not drop. When the pudding is cooked, drain it, untie the cloth and turn it out on to a serving platter, removing the cloth. When ready to serve, warm the rest of the brandy, pour it over the pudding and set it alight.

Hard Sauce

Sauce pour le pudding

Serves 12

175 g/6 oz unsalted butter
2 egg yolks
3 tablespoons sifted icing sugar
2 tablespoons rum

Combine the ingredients in a double boiler. Stir until the mixture thickens and serve it hot.

Baked Peaches

Croûtes aux pêches

Serves 6

6 slices bread, crusts removed
3 ripe peaches, halved and stoned
6 tablespoons granulated sugar
125 g/4 oz unsalted butter, cut into 6 pieces

Preheat the oven to 170°C/325°F/mark 3. Generously butter a 20-cm/8-inch pie dish. Arrange the slices of bread in it. Place half a peach, cut side uppermost, on each slice of bread. In the cavity left by the stone, sprinkle 1 tablespoon granulated sugar and 1 piece of unsalted butter.

Bake for 20 minutes or until cooked through. Serve warm or cold.

Upside Down Apple Tart

Tarte Tatin

Serves 8

225 g/8 oz plain flour
65 g/2½ oz icing sugar
1/8 teaspoon salt
1 egg yolk
225 g/8 oz unsalted butter, cut into pieces
6 russet apples, peeled and sliced

Pour the flour into a bowl, make a well in the centre and in it put half the sugar, the salt, the egg yolk and 125 ml/4 fl oz warm water. Mix well, then add half the butter.

Knead the dough until smooth, then roll it out into a rectangle. Fold up the rectangle, cover it with a damp cloth and leave to rest for 1 hour. Roll out the dough again into a round 5 mm/¼ inch thick.

Preheat the oven to 200°C/400°F/mark 6. Arrange the apple slices in a deep pie dish. Add the rest of the pieces of butter, and sprinkle with the rest of the sugar. Cover with the dough. Bake for 45 minutes. Turn the tart out on to a plate so that the pastry is on top.

Pound Cake

Quatre-quarts

The French name for pound cake is 'four quarters' because this cake uses equal weights of the four main ingredients.

Serves 8

5 eggs, separated
About 175 g/6 oz unsalted butter
About 175 g/6 oz granulated sugar
About 175 g/6 oz plain flour
1 teaspoon grated lemon rind

Preheat the oven to 180°C/350°F/mark 4. Butter a deep 20-cm/8-inch cake tin. Weigh the eggs and weigh out the same weight of butter, sugar and flour. Melt the butter gently. When it begins to melt, remove it from the heat. Beat the egg yolks with the sugar in a bowl with the grated rind. When the mixture turns pale, add the melted butter. Mix well. Gradually beat in the flour. Beat the egg whites into stiff peaks. When the mixture is smooth, incorporate the egg whites, folding them in gently. Pour the mixture into the prepared cake tin and bake for 1 hour.

Melanie's Puff Pastry Cheesecake

Galette feuilletée (Mélanie)

Serves 8

225 g/8 oz plain flour
½ teaspoon salt
125 g/4 oz unsalted butter , softened
125 g/4 oz curd or cream cheese, at room temperature
1 egg, beaten

Sift the flour into a bowl. Make a well in the centre and pour 4 tablespoons warm water, and the salt, into it. Gradually incorporate the water and salt into the flour to make a dough. Knead the flour into a ball. Cover with a damp cloth and leave to rest for 30 minutes. Beat the softened butter and the cheese together.

Roll out the dough into a rectangle about 5 mm/¼ inch thick. Place the butter and cheese mixture in the centre and fold the dough over it. Roll it with a rolling pin several times, then fold the dough in half and in half again. Give it a quarter turn and roll it out again. Repeat, giving the dough another quarter turn, then leave it to rest for 15 minutes. Do this a total of eight times, giving it 6 quarter turns.

Preheat the oven to 190°C/375°F/mark 5. Roll out the dough to fit a 20-cm/8-inch round pie dish. It should not be too thick, about the thickness of a finger. Bake for 30 minutes or until golden.

Mélanie's Soufflé Fritters

Beignets soufflés ou Pets-de-nonne (Mélanie)

Makes about 12

250 ml/8 fl oz milk
1/8 teaspoon salt
¼ teaspoon granulated sugar
125 g/4 oz unsalted butter
1 tablespoon brandy
125 g/4 oz plain flour
4 eggs
500 ml/16 fl oz vegetable oil
125 g/4 oz icing sugar, sifted

Heat the milk in a saucepan with the salt, sugar, butter, and brandy. As soon as the liquid boils, add the flour. Place the pan half off the heat and beat the mixture well with a wooden spoon until it is smooth. When it starts to leave the sides of the pan without sticking to the spoon, remove the pan from the heat. Break the eggs into it, beating until smooth after each addition. The dough should be soft but not liquid.

Leave the dough to rest for 1 hour. Heat the oil in a deep frying-pan. Shape the dough into small balls and deep-fry them. Increase the heat as the fritters swell. When they are nicely puffed up and browned, remove them with a skimmer, drain them on absorbent kitchen paper and transfer them to a serving dish. When all are cooked sprinkle them with the icing sugar.

Chocolate Gâteau

Gâteau au chocolat

Serves 8

2 eggs
About 50 g/2 oz unsalted butter
About 50 g/2 oz bitter chocolate
About 50 g/2 oz icing sugar
2 tablespoons plain flour

Weigh the eggs in their shells. Weigh out an equal amount of butter, chocolate and icing sugar. Melt the chocolate in a small pan with 2 tablespoons water. Remove from the heat and beat in the butter. When the mixture is smooth leave it to cool. Preheat the oven to 170°C/325°F/mark 3.

Separate the eggs. Beat the yolks and stir them into the mixture. Then beat in the icing sugar and the flour. Whip the egg whites into stiff peaks and fold them into the mixture. Pour the mixture into a well-buttered 20-cm/8-inch cake tin and bake for 20 minutes.

Chocolate Cobblestone Cake

Pavé au chocolat

Serves 6

225 g/8 oz bitter chocolate
125 g/4 oz unsalted butter
1 egg
12 trifle sponge cakes, split in half horizontally

Melt the chocolate over very low heat with 3 tablespoons water. Stir it and when it is completely smooth, beat in the butter. Beat the whole egg and stir it into the mixture. Have a pan of warm water ready on the stove.

Spread some of the chocolate mixture on 12 cake halves on a dish. Top with the other cake halves.

Place three of the cakes vertically side-by-side on a serving dish. Cover them with the chocolate cream. Then arrange three more cakes next to them but horizontally. Cover them with the cream. Add the next three facing in

the original direction, below the second set, and complete the square with three more cakes laid horizontally below the first vertical group. You should now have a large square. Spread with any remaining chocolate cream to cover any gaps and smooth with a warmed metal spatula. If the cream becomes too stiff to spread while you are working, dip the bowl in the pan of warm water that is ready on the heat.

Strawberry mousse

Mousse aux fraises

Serves 4

450 g/1 lb strawberries
50 g/2 oz sifted icing sugar
4 egg whites

Push the strawberries through a sieve. Mix the strawberry juice with the icing sugar . Preheat the oven to 150°C/300°F/mark 2. Butter a pie dish. Beat the egg whites into very stiff peaks and carefully fold the strawberry juice into them. Pour the mixture into the pan and bake for 10 minutes. Serve immediately.

Mocha Cream

Crème moka

Serves 8

6 egg yolks
225 g/8 oz plain flour
225 g/8 oz granulated sugar
225 g/8 oz unsalted butter, softened
About 250 ml/8 fl oz strong black coffee

Beat the yolks, in a bowl with the flour, sugar and softened butter. Pour in the coffee, beating constantly. When the coffee no longer mixes into the cream, stop pouring. Cook the mixture, stirring constantly with a wooden spoon, for 10 minutes on low heat.

Vanilla Cream

Crème à la vanille

Serves 8

1 litre/1¾ pints milk
2.5-cm/1-inch piece vanilla bean
225 g/8 oz granulated sugar
6 egg yolks
2 eggs

Preheat the oven to 150°C/300°F/gas 2. Boil the milk with the vanilla bean and sugar for 10 minutes. Remove the milk from the heat and cool slightly before beating in the egg yolks and whole eggs. Beat with a wire whisk. Strain the mixture through a fine sieve and pour it into a baking dish. Place the baking dish in a large roasting tin half-filled with water. Bake for 30 minutes or until the cream is set.

Chestnut Cake

Gâteau de marrons

Serves 12

1 litre/1¾ pints milk
225 g/8 oz granulated sugar
1 vanilla bean
1 kg/2¼ lb peeled chestnuts
175 g/6 oz butter, softened
6 eggs, separated

Butter a charlotte mould. Heat the milk with the sugar and vanilla bean. Stir until the sugar has dissolved, then bring to the boil. Add the chestnuts and cook for about 30 minutes, or until they are soft. Remove and drain them. Push them through a sieve. Beat the butter into the chestnuts. When the purée has cooled to lukewarm, stir in the egg yolks, one after the other, beating well after each addition.

Preheat the oven to 170°C/325°F/mark 3. Whip the egg whites into stiff peaks and fold them into the purée. Pour the mixture into a charlotte mould. Set the mould in a baking tin filled with warm water and bake for 30 minutes. Remove from the heat and leave it to cool. Serve the cake well chilled.

Genoese Sponge

Génoise

Serves 8

3 eggs
2 egg yolks
125 g/4 oz caster sugar
125 g/4 oz plain flour, sifted
125 g/4 oz unsalted butter, melted
3 teaspoons rum

Butter a 20 cm/8 in sponge tin or moule à manqué, line it with greaseproof paper and butter the paper.

Place the eggs, egg yolks and sugar in a bowl over 5 cm/2 inches of water barely simmering in a saucepan, or in a double boiler. Whisk them for at least 10 minutes until very thick, light and lukewarm. Remove from the water and continue whisking a further five minutes or more, until it leaves a trail on the surface when the beaters are lifted.

Preheat the oven to 180°C/350°F/mark 4. Sift a little of the flour into the egg and sugar mixture and fold it in carefully using a metal spoon. Gradually add the rest of the flour in the same way, and then the rum, beating until the mixture is smooth. Fold in the melted butter a spoonful at a time.

Pour into the prepared tin and bake for 20-25 minutes or until a knife inserted in the centre comes out clean.

Flat Cake

Galette

Serves 8

225 g/8 oz plain flour
2 teaspoons salt
225 g/8 oz unsalted butter
125 ml/4 fl oz milk
1 egg, beaten

Combine all the ingredients except the egg to form a dough. Sprinkle a work surface with flour and roll out the dough into a rectangle. Fold it over on itself and leave it to rest under a damp cloth for 15 minutes. Do this three times, giving the dough a quarter turn each time, and leaving it to rest under a damp cloth for 15 minutes.

Roll out the dough into a large circle and lay it on a greased baking sheet. Preheat the oven to 180°C/350°F/mark 4. Use a sharp knife to trace a lattice pattern on the dough. Brush the dough with the beaten egg. Bake for 30 minutes or until golden.

Apple Fritters

Beignets de pommes

Serves 6

125 g/4 oz plain flour
2 egg yolks
1 tablespoon brandy
¼ teaspoon salt
About 125 ml/4 fl oz milk
6 russet apples
500 ml/16 fl oz oil
225 g/8 oz granulated sugar

Pour the flour into a bowl and make a well in the centre. Into it, put the egg yolks, brandy and salt. Gradually incorporate the flour, then add enough milk to make a smooth, fairly thick batter. Leave it to rest for at least 20 minutes.

Peel the apples, core and slice them and put them into the batter. Heat the oil in a frying-pan and deep-fry the apple slices. Drain them and sprinkle with the sugar.

Upside Down Cream

Crème renversée

Serves 6

1 litre/1¾ pints milk
225 g/8 oz icing sugar
2.5-cm/1-inch piece of vanilla bean
6 eggs, beaten

Rinse a mould in cold water. Boil the milk with 350 g/12 oz of the sugar and the vanilla bean. Remove from the heat, discard the vanilla bean and leave to cool. Beat the eggs into the milk. Make a caramel by melting the rest of the sugar with 2 tablespoons water in a heavy-based pan and allowing it to boil. As it begins to colour, quickly pour it into the mould and turn the mould to coat the bottom and sides evenly. Leave it to cool, then pour in the egg-and-milk mixture.

Preheat the oven to 180°C/350°F/mark 4. Set the mould in a pan half-filled with warm water and place it in the oven. Bake for 30 minutes or until set. Remove and leave to cool.

When the cream is firm, turn it out on to a dish.

Cream to Accompany Rice Pudding

Crème pour accompagner le pudding au riz

Serves 6

40 g/1½ oz unsalted butter
3 tablespoons granulated sugar
2 egg yolks, beaten
Juice of ½ lemon
125 ml/4 fl oz sherry

In a small saucepan, melt the butter over low heat and stir in the sugar. Add the beaten egg yolks, stirring until the mixture is light and fluffy. Continue beating with a wooden spoon while adding 2 tablespoons hot water.

Put the saucepan into a larger saucepan containing hot water. Beat with a whisk, while adding the lemon juice and sherry. Cook for 5 minutes. Serve warm.

Fried Custard Creams

Crème frite

Makes about 10 pieces

65 g/2½ oz plain flour
250 ml/8 fl oz boiling milk
4 eggs
2 tablespoons granulated sugar
1 egg white, lightly beaten
125 g/4 oz dry cake crumbs
125 ml/4 fl oz vegetable oil or unsalted butter

Combine the flour and boiling milk, beating well. Leave to cool. Beat the eggs and sugar into the dough. Transfer the mixture to a saucepan and cook, stirring with a wooden spoon, for 30 minutes. Pour the dough on to a wetted marble slab and roll it out until it is the thickness of a finger. Leave it to cool. When cold, cut it into diamonds, rounds, and rectangles.

Heat the oil or butter in a frying-pan. Dip the creams into the beaten egg white and then into the cake crumbs. Fry them until they are golden.

Cherry Bake

Clafouti

Reserve the cherry stones for adding to other baked or stewed fruit to give it a good flavour.

Serves 4

125 g/4 oz plain flour
75 g/3 oz icing sugar
2 eggs
1/8 teaspoon salt
300 ml/10 fl oz milk
25 g/1 oz unsalted butter
450 g/1 lb cherries, stoned

Preheat the oven to 190°C/375°F/mark 5. Make a batter with the flour, 2 tablespoons of the sugar, the eggs, salt and the milk. The batter should be smooth but not be too liquid. Butter a pie dish and put the cherries into it; they should be tightly packed. Pour the batter over them and sprinkle with the rest of the sugar. Bake for about 45 minutes or until the batter is golden.

Chestnut Soufflé

Soufflé aux marrons

Dried chestnuts can be used for this recipe, but they may need longer cooking.

Serves 6

450 g/1 lb peeled chestnuts
500 ml/16 fl oz milk
2.5-cm/1-inch piece vanilla bean
125 g/4 oz granulated sugar
3 eggs, separated

Put the chestnuts into a saucepan and add the milk, vanilla bean and sugar. Simmer over low heat, uncovered, for 30 minutes or until the chestnuts are softened. Drain the chestnuts, reserving the cooking liquid. Discard the vanilla bean. Purée the chestnuts. Put the purée into a bowl and stir in the cooking liquid. Preheat the oven to 180°C/350°F/mark 4. When the mixture is smooth beat in the egg yolks, one at a time. Beat the egg whites into stiff peaks, then delicately fold them into the chestnut mixture.

Pour the mixture into a buttered soufflé dish. Bake for 30 to 40 minutes or until well risen and lightly browned on top.

Soufflé Omelette

Omelette soufflée

Serves 4

6 eggs, separated
275 g/10 oz granulated sugar
1 teaspoon grated lemon rind
15 g/½ oz unsalted butter

Beat the yolks with 6 tablespoons of the sugar and the grated rind. Beat the egg whites into very stiff peaks, then beat in 1 tablespoon sugar.

Preheat the oven to 190°C/375°F/mark 5. Fold the whites into the yolks. Melt the butter in an ovenproof dish and pour the mixture into it. Sprinkle the rest of the sugar over the top. Bake for 6 to 8 minutes or until lightly browned. Serve immediately, as it sinks quickly.

Apricot Charlotte

Charlotte aux abricots

Serves 8

1 kg/2¼ lb sponge fingers
4 tablespoons kirsch
225 g/8 oz apricot jam, warmed

Dip the sponge fingers in the kirsch and use them to line the bottom and sides of a charlotte mould . Fill any gaps with broken sponge fingers. Spread them with a layer of jam. Arrange another layer of sponge fingers on top of the first, and at right angles to it. Spread it with the jam. Continue layering and spreading with jam until the mould is full. Cover with a tight-fitting lid and place a weight on top of it. Leave in a cool place. Serve with vanilla custard.

Swiss Roll

Biscuit roulé

Serves 6

125 g/4 oz granulated sugar
4 eggs, separated
75 g/3 oz plain flour
1 tablespoon rum
225 g/8 oz apricot jam

Caramel glaze

125 g/4 oz granulated sugar

Butter a sheet of greaseproof paper large enough to fit a baking sheet. Preheat the oven to 170°C/325°F/mark 3. Beat the sugar with the egg yolks for 10 minutes. Gradually add the flour, then add the rum. Whip the egg whites into stiff peaks and fold them gently into the mixture. Turn the mixture out on to the greaseproof paper. Bake for about 30 minutes, or until the cake begins to turn golden.

Remove the cake from the oven and leave it to cool slightly. Place a cloth over a marble work surface and turn the cake out, papered side upwards, on to the cloth. Remove the paper. Spread the jam evenly over the cake. Use the cloth to help you roll up the cake while it is still hot. Leave it to cool.

To make the caramel glaze, heat 250 ml/8 fl oz water and the sugar in a heavy-based pan. Bring to the bbboil without stirring and do not stir when boiling. As soon as the syrup begins to colour, pour the caramel glaze over the Swiss roll.

Baked Apples

Pommes au beurre

Serves 4

4 slices day-old bread
4 cooking apples, peeled and cored
125 g/4 oz unsalted butter
225 g/8 oz granulated sugar
4 tablespoons blackcurrant jam

Preheat the oven to 200°C/400°F/mark 6. Butter a shallow baking dish. Cut the bread into circles the same size of the apples. Lay the bread circles on the dish and arrange the apples on the bread. Cut half the butter into four small pieces and put each one in the hole in the centre of an apple. Bake for 10 minutes, then put a teaspoon of sugar into the hole. Bake for another 10 minutes.

Combine four tablespoons sugar with the rest of the butter. Divide in four and fill the holes with the mixture. Bake for 1 hour in all. Just before serving, fill the holes in the centres of the apples with blackcurrant jam.

Apricot Soufflé

Soufflé à l'abricot

Serves 8

8 egg whites
375-g/13-ounce jar apricot jam

Preheat the oven to 130°C/250°F/mark ½. Whip the egg whites into stiff peaks. Gradually fold them into the apricot jam. Pour the mixture into a buttered soufflé dish and bake for 1½ hours. If the oven is too hot the soufflé will not rise.

Savoy Sponge Cake

Biscuit de Savoie

Serves 6

6 eggs, separated
75 g/3 oz icing sugar, sifted
75 g/3 oz plain flour, sifted
25 g/1 oz unsalted butter

Butter a deep 20-cm/8-inch cake tin. Preheat the oven to 170°C/325°F/mark 3. Beat the egg yolks with the sugar until the mixture turns pale. Gradually beat in the flour. Beat the egg whites into stiff peaks and fold them into the mixture. Bake for about 50 minutes or until a knife inserted into the cake comes out clean.

Stewed Peaches

Pêches à la Bourdaloue

Serves 6

6 large, ripe peaches
350 g/12 oz granulated sugar
1 vanilla bean
4 macaroons, crushed
25 g/1 oz unsalted butter, cut into pieces

Pastry Cream

6 egg yolks
125 g/4 oz granulated sugar
1 tablespoon plain flour
500 ml/16 fl oz milk

Place the peaches in boiling water to blanch them and loosen the skins. Peel them, cut them in half and stone them. Put the sugar, 500 ml/16 fl oz water, and the vanilla bean into a heavy pan and bring to the boil, stirring only until the sugar dissolves. Boil the syrup for 5 minutes then add the peach halves. Remove the pan from the heat, leaving the peaches to soak in the syrup.

To make the pastry cream, beat the egg yolks with 2 tablespoons of the sugar and the flour. Boil the milk and gradually beat it into the mixture. Transfer the mixture to a saucepan and heat it, stirring constantly. As soon as it boils, remove it from the heat. When it is cold, spread half of it over the bottom of an ovenproof dish. Drain the peaches and arrange them on top. Then cover with another layer of pastry cream. Refrigerate while you make the brittle.

Melt the remaining sugar in a dry frying-pan. As soon as the sugar colours, remove the pan from the heat and stir in the crushed macaroons. Remove the pan from the heat and pour the mixture out on to a wetted baking sheet. Leave to cool. When cold, crush this brittle with a rolling pin. Sprinkle the mixture over the custard and dot with the butter.

Preheat the oven to 180°C/350°F/mark 4. Bake for about 15 minutes, or until the brittle melts and coats the custard. Serve warm.

Brioche with Greengages

Brioches aux reines-claudes

Serves 6

6 slices brioche
50 g/2 oz unsalted butter
450 g/1 lb greengages, halved and stoned
50 g/2 oz icing sugar

Preheat the oven to 180°C/350°F/mark 4. Butter the slices of brioche and arrange them in a buttered ovenproof dish. Cover them with the halved greengages, then sprinkle with the icing sugar. Bake for 15 minutes.

Fried Apples

Pommes frites

Serves 4

4 apples, peeled, cored, and sliced
125 ml/4 fl oz brandy
4 tablespoons sifted icing sugar
125 g/4 oz plain flour
125 g/4 oz unsalted butter

Marinate the apple slices in the brandy and icing sugar for several hours. Drain them and dip them in flour. Melt the butter in a frying-pan and fry the apple slices until golden.

Rich Chocolate Cream

Crème somptueuse

Prepare this cream 24 hours in advance so that it sets well. It can be kept in the refrigerator for two or three days.

Serves 6

350 g/12 ounces bitter chocolate
125 g/4 oz unsalted butter, cut into pieces
3 egg yolks

In a saucepan over very low heat or in a double boiler, dissolve the chocolate in 3 tablespoons water. Stir with a wooden spoon and when the chocolate is creamy, remove the pan from the heat. Beat in the butter, 1 piece at a time, until the mixture is smooth. Whisk the egg yolks in a bowl. Beat in the chocolate mixture gradually with a wooden spoon, until you have a smooth cream. Turn it into a serving bowl.

Burnt Cream

Crème brûlée

Serves 4

250 ml/8 fl oz double cream or crème fraîche
6 egg yolks
2 tablespoons granulated sugar
4 tablespoons crushed brittle or brown sugar

Pour the cream into a saucepan and stand it in a larger saucepan of hot water, or use a double boiler. Heat until the cream turns liquid but do not let it boil.

Beat the egg yolks with the granulated sugar until the mixture foams. Add the liquified cream. Pour it into a large mould ; it should be two fingers deep.

Preheat the oven to 190°C/375°F/mark 5. Set the mould in a roasting tin half-filled with warm water and place it in the oven. Bake for 30 minutes or until set.

Leave the cream to cool in a cold place. Sprinkle it with the crushed brittle or brown sugar and place it under a preheated grill to melt the topping and form a caramel crust. Leave to cool and serve cold.

Baked Bananas

Bananes au gratin

Serves 6

6 bananas
40 g/1½ oz icing sugar
2 tablespoons lemon juice
2 tablespoons melted unsalted butter

Preheat the oven to 200°C/400°F/mark 6. Slice the bananas in four lengthways. Arrange them in a shallow buttered oven dish. Combine the icing sugar, lemon juice and butter and pour half of this sauce over the bananas. Bake for 20 minutes, basting with the rest of the sauce every 5 minutes. Serve hot or cold.

Cherry Bread

Pain de cerises

Serves 4

65 g/2½ oz plain flour
¼ teaspoon salt
450 g/1 lb cherries, stoned
125 g/4 oz unsalted butter, cut into small cubes

Preheat the oven to 190°C/375°F/mark 5. Combine the flour, 500 ml/16 fl oz water and the salt. Mix this with the cherries. Butter a shallow ovenproof dish and pour the mixture into it. Sprinkle with the little cubes of butter. Bake for just under 1 hour or until browned.

Apples with Pistachios

Pommes aux pistaches

Serves 6

225 g/8 oz granulated sugar
1 vanilla bean
6 tart eating apples, peeled and cored
150 g/5 oz pistachio nuts, shelled and peeled

Heat the sugar and 250 ml/8 fl oz water in a heavy pan. Add the vanilla bean. When the syrup boils, add the apples. Cook, basting with the syrup, for 10 minutes. Remove the apples and let them cool before placing them on a serving dish . Stick the pistachio nuts into the apples. Continue cooking the syrup until it thickens but do not let it colour. Pour it over the apples. Leave to cool and serve cold.

Apple Meringue

Pommes meringuées

Serves 6

10 cooking apples, peeeled, cored and sliced
225 g/8 oz stoned prunes (optional)
225 g/8 oz granulated sugar
2 egg whites
1 tablespoon grated lemon rind

Preheat the oven to 150°C/300°F/mark 2. Stew the apples, with the prunes if used, and 200 g/7 oz of the sugar in 250 ml/8 fl oz water until cooked but still firm, about 10 minutes. Pour the stewed apples into an ovenproof dish, mounding them into a pyramid. Beat the egg whites, and when they form soft peaks, beat in the rest of the sugar and the lemon rind. Pile this meringue on top of the apples. Bake for 15 minutes or until the meringue is firm and beginning to colour. Serve hot.

Chocolate Creams

Crème au chocolat

Serves 6

1.1 litres/2 pints milk
225 g/ 8 oz grated bitter chocolate
75 g/3 oz granulated sugar
5 egg yolks
1 egg

Pour 125 ml/4 fl oz of the milk into a saucepan and heat it over low heat. Add the grated chocolate and stir to melt. Gradually add the rest of the milk and the sugar, stirring constantly with a wooden spoon. Remove the mixture from the heat and leave it to cool. Beat the

yolks with the whole egg and beat this into the mixture. Strain the mixture through muslin or a fine sieve.

Preheat the oven to 180°C/350°F/gas 4. Pour the cream into 6 dariole moulds. Set these in a pan half-filled with warm water and place them in the oven. Bake for 30 minutes or until set.

Flamed Apples

Pommes flambées

Serves 4

225 g/8 oz granulated sugar
4 apples, peeled and cored
4 tablespoons raspberry or blackcurrant jam
4 tablespoons cognac, warmed

Put the sugar and 250 ml/8 fl oz water into a heavy pan and bring to the boil without stirring. When the syrup has boiled for 5 minutes, add the apples. Cook for 10 minutes. Remove the apples, continuing to cook the syrup, and place them on the serving dish. Fill the holes in the centre with the preserves. Reduce the syrup for another 10 minutes until it has thickened but not coloured and pour it over the apples. Pour the warmed cognac over them and set it alight.

Bananas in Red Wine

Daube de bananes

Serves 6

50 g/2 oz unsalted butter
6 bananas, split lengthways
750 ml/1¼ pints dry red wine
3 tablespoons sifted icing sugar
¼ teaspoon ground cinnamon

Melt the butter in a frying-pan and add the bananas. Fry them until they are golden, turning them to cook them on both sides. Remove and reserve them. Boil the wine in a large saucepan with the icing sugar and cinnamon on medium to low heat for 10 minutes. Add the bananas and simmer for 10 minutes. Serve hot.

Banana Ice Cream

La glace à la banane

Serves 6

500 ml/16 fl oz milk
¼ teaspoon salt
5 egg yolks
225 g/ 8 oz sifted icing sugar
1 teaspoon cornflour
4 bananas
175 g/6 fl oz double cream or crème fraîche

At least 15 minutes before it is required, prepare a hand-cranked ice cream maker, by filling it with layers of crushed ice and sea-salt with a little saltpetre.

To make the basic mixture, boil the milk with a pinch of salt. Meanwhile, put the egg yolks, sugar and cornflour into a bowl. Beat well with a wooden spoon until the mixture is white and foaming. Incorporate a little of the boiling milk, while stirring. Pour the mixture into a copper pan and add the rest of the milk. Cook on low heat, stirring constantly, until the mixture thickens but do not let it boil. As soon as the mixture coats the back of a spoon, remove it from the heat. Leave it to cool.

Peel the bananas and mash them with a fork to make a purée. Pass them through a fine sieve. Incorporate this purée into the cooled mixture. Gradually add the cream, beating gently with a wire whisk.

Pour the mixture into the ice cream maker. Cover it with a circle of waxed paper then add the lid. Crank the handle of the ice cream maker for 30 minutes until the ice cream begins to freeze.

Open the ice cream maker and remove the frozen mixture. Press it into the mould you have chosen to use, preferably a sugarloaf-shaped (conical) mould. Pack the ice cream in, using a wooden spoon to remove air pockets. Cover the open end of the mould with a circle of waxed paper. Place.it in a narrow bucket partly filled with ice and salt. Leave for 1 hour to set.

Just before serving, remove the mould from the bucket, hold it under cold water, then dip it into hot water. Turn it out onto a napkin on the serving dish.

To Preserve Whole Bunches of Grapes

Pour conserver les grappes de raisins

Hang each bunch from a string, outdoors if it is sunny, and, if not, in the storeroom. They need heat and no humidity. If they are preserved indoors, they need to be well aired. Remove any grapes which are damaged.

To Make Raisins from Grapes

Pour sêcher les raisins

Boil a handful of wood ash in water to cover for 2 hours. Filter the water through muslin. Return it to the heat to boil it until it is reduced. Dip undamaged grapes in it. Begin with just one bunch, and if the grapes do not wrinkle up immediately, boil the water for longer. Rinse the grapes in cold water, then hang them up in a dry, airy place. When the raisins are to be used, wash them in fresh water several times and then leave them to swell in warm water.

Opposite: Banana ice cream was served after the huge Christmas lunch (recipe on this page).

Teas

Chestnut Biscuits

Galettes aux marrons

Makes 18

125 g/4 oz unsalted butter
225 g/8 oz unsweetened chestnut purée
175 g/6 oz granulated sugar
3 eggs, separated

Butter three 6-cup bun tins. Preheat the oven to 180°C/350°F/mark 4. Melt the butter over low heat and stir in the chestnut purée, sugar and egg yolks. Remove the pan from the heat. Beat the egg whites into stiff peaks and gently fold them in. Divide the mixture among the moulds. Bake for 20 minutes, or until firm.

Genoa Cake

Pain de Gênes

Serves 8

125g/4 oz unsalted butter, softened
175g/6 oz icing sugar
5 eggs
275 g/10 oz ground almonds
2 tablespoons kirsch
75g/3 oz plain flour
50 g/2 oz sifted icing sugar (optional)
125 g/4 oz slivered almonds (optional)

Butter a 20-cm/8-inch sponge tin or moule à manqué. Preheat the oven to 180°C/350°F/mark 4. Cream the butter in a bowl and beat in the icing sugar until the mixture is creamy. Continue beating while incorporating the eggs, one at a time, beating well after each addition. Beat in the ground almonds with the kirsch. Add the flour and beat well. Pour into the prepared tin and bake for 40 minutes or until golden.

If liked, sprinkle with sifted icing sugar and top with slivered almonds.

Rich Fruit Cake

Cake

Serves 8

40 g/1½ oz unsalted butter
3 tablespoons granulated sugar
2 eggs
2 tablespoons rum
225 g/8 oz mixed dried fruit, chopped
150 g/5 oz plain flour

Butter a 20-cm/8-inch cake tin. Preheat the oven to 170°C/325°/mark 3. Soften the butter in a bain-marie or double boiler. Remove the bowl from the heat and beat in the sugar. Add the eggs one after the other, beating well after each addition. Add the rum and the dried fruit. Gradually beat in the flour. Turn the mixture into the cake tin and bake for at least 20 minutes, or until a knife inserted into the centre comes out clean.

Scones

Scones

Makes about 20

225 g/8 oz plain flour
1 teaspoon baking powder
¼ teaspoon salt
50 g/2 oz butter
About 150 ml/5 fl oz milk

Sift the flour with the baking powder and salt. Rub in the butter. Add enough milk to make a soft dough. Roll out the dough to 1 cm/½ inch thick.

Preheat the oven to 200°C/400°F/mark 6. Cut out circles with a biscuit cutter and place them on a buttered baking sheet. Bake for 15 minutes or until well-risen and lightly browned.

Serve hot with butter.

Opposite: Monet's favourite teatime cakes were scones, chestnut biscuits, Genoa cake and rich fruit cake (recipes on this page).

179

Honey Biscuits

Palets au miel

Makes 15

2 eggs
100g/3½ oz icing sugar
50 g/2 oz honey
150 g/5 oz plain flour

Combine the eggs and sugar, beating hard for at least 5 minutes. Add the honey and mix well, then beat in the flour gradually. Leave the mixture to rest for 30 minutes.

Butter a baking sheet. Preheat the oven to 150°C/300°F/mark 2. Use a teaspoon to place small mounds of the mixture on the baking sheet. Bake for 15 minutes, or until the biscuits are golden-brown.

Millet's Bread Rolls

Petits pains (Millet)

Makes 29

250 ml/8 fl oz milk
5 teaspoons granulated sugar or 8 to 10 sugar lumps
1 teaspoon salt
40 g/1½ oz unsalted butter
1 tablespoon fresh yeast
450 g/1 lb strong, plain flour
2 eggs, beaten
1 egg yolk, mixed with 3 tablespoons milk

Heat the milk with the sugar to just below the boil. Leave it to cool to lukewarm. Add the salt and butter. Meanwhile, in a bowl sprinkle the yeast over 250 ml/8 fl oz warm water. Stir in 4 tablespoons of the flour. Leave in a warm place for 20 minutes, by which time the mixture should be spongy. Add the rest of the flour.

Mix the lukewarm milk mixture with the eggs. Beat the mixture into the flour mixture and beat with a wooden spoon, then knead by hand, until the dough is smooth and elastic, and no longer sticks to the sides of the bowl.

Sprinkle flour on a board and knead the dough on it for another 5 minutes. Use a warmed knife to cut the dough into 29 pieces and roll each of these into a fat sausage shape, about 1 inch by 3 inches. Place the pieces of dough in a warm place in the kitchen, cover with a damp cloth and leave for 3 hours.

Preheat the oven to 230°C/450°F/mark 8. Flour 2 baking sheets. Place the pieces of dough on the baking sheets and brush them with the egg yolk and milk mixture. Bake for 10 minutes.

Cinnamon Toast

Toasts à la canelle

Makes 12

175 g/6 oz unsalted butter, softened
175g/6 oz granulated sugar
5 teaspoons ground cinnamon
12 slices bread

Preheat the oven to 230°C/450°F/mark 8. Work the butter, sugar, and ground cinnamon into a smooth paste. Spread the mixture evenly over the slices of bread. Arrange the slices on a baking sheet and bake for 10 minutes, or until the butter bubbles. Serve hot.

Orange Cake

Gâteau à l'orange

Serves 6-8

125 g/4 oz granulated sugar
2 eggs, separated
Juice of 1 orange, strained
125 g/4 oz ground almonds
75 g/3 oz plain flour

Butter a 20cm/8-inch cake tin. Preheat the oven to 170°C/325°F/mark 3. Beat the sugar and egg yolks together so that the mixture foams. Gradually beat in the strained orange juice, almonds and flour. Beat the egg whites into stiff peaks and incorporate them into the mixture. Pour the mixture into the cake tin and bake for 30 minutes or until a knife inserted in the centre of the cake comes out clean.

Madeleines

Madeleines au citron

Makes 12

250 g/9 oz granulated sugar
125 g/4 oz unsalted butter, softened
4 eggs, separated
125 g/4 oz plain flour
Grated rind of 1 lemon

Lightly butter and flour 12 madeleine moulds. In a bowl, combine the sugar, butter and egg yolks. Beat well until the mixture turns pale. Beat the egg whites into soft peaks. Gradually add the butter-and-egg mixture to the whites, alternately with 1 tablespoon of the flour, until the mixture and the flour are used up.

Preheat the oven to 200°C/400°F/mark 6. Place a teaspoon of the mixture in each mould.

Bake for 10 to 15 minutes, but no longer, or the madeleines will be too dry.

Caroline's Pancakes

Crêpes (Caroline)

The eggs can be separated and the whites beaten into peaks before incorporating them into the batter.

Serves 10

225 g/8 oz plain flour
About 250 ml/8 fl oz milk
About 3 eggs
1 tablespoon vegetable oil
125 g/4 oz unsalted butter

Make the batter 3 hours ahead of time, combining all the ingredients except the butter. If it seems too thin, add an egg; if it seems too thick add more milk.

To cook the pancakes, heat an omelette or crêpe pan over high heat and melt 15 g/½ oz butter in it, shaking the pan to coat it evenly. Drop enough batter into the pan to make 1 thin pancake and cook quickly. Flip the pancake over with a metal spatula or fishslice. Turn out on to a dish and reserve in a warm place. Continue until all the butter and batter are used up.

Almond Biscuits

Gâteaux nantais

Makes 40

450 g/1 lb plain flour
225 g/8 oz icing sugar
125g/4 oz unsalted butter , softened
125 g/4 oz ground almonds
Grated rind of 1 lemon
4 eggs
75 g/3 oz chopped almonds for garnish
225g/8 oz granulated sugar

Butter two baking sheets. Preheat the oven to 170°C/325°F/mark 3. Pour the flour into a bowl and make a well in the centre. Pour the icing sugar into the well, and add the butter, ground almonds, lemon rind and eggs. Mix well. When the dough is smooth but firm, roll it out on a floured work surface into a rectangle about 1 cm/½ inch thick. Cut the dough into rounds with a biscuit cutter. Transfer the biscuits to the baking sheets, and sprinkle them with the chopped almonds and the sugar. Bake for about 20 minutes or until golden.

Poor Knights

Pain perdu

Serves 4

2 eggs, beaten
125 ml/4 fl oz milk
2 tablespoons sifted icing sugar
2 tablespoons rum
4 slices day-old brioche
50 g/2 oz unsalted butter
125 g/4 oz granulated sugar

Pour the beaten eggs into a shallow bowl. Combine the milk with the icing sugar and rum. Pour it into another shallow bowl. Soak the slices of brioche in the milk mixture. As soon as they are soaked (do not wait for them to soften), dip the slices on both sides in the egg.

Melt the butter in a frying-pan. Fry the slices in the butter, until browned on both sides. Serve hot, generously sprinkled with the granulated sugar.

Jams

Plum Jam

Confiture de prunes

Apricot jam can be made in the same way as plum jam.

Makes about 750 g/1 lb 10 oz

750 g/1 ½ lb granulated sugar
450 g/1 lb plums, halved and stoned

Pour the sugar and 125 ml/4 fl oz water into a copper preserving pan. Bring to the boil, stirring only until the sugar has dissolved. Boil for 5 minutes, then add enough plums to cover the bottom of the pan. They are cooked when they are transparent and when they will soften when pressed with the handle of a wooden spoon.

Remove the pan from the heat, and use a fork to remove the plums from the pan. Place them in preserving jars. Return the pan to the heat and bring the syrup to a rolling boil again. Place more plums in the pan, and repeat the procedure until all the plums are used up. Put the syrup back on the heat and pour any syrup in the jars back into the pan. Boil it again and pour it into the pots, being sure to dislodge the plums so that the syrup penetrates everywhere.

Uncooked Redcurrant Jelly

Gelée de groseille à froid

Makes about 750 g/1 lb 10 oz

450 g/1 lb redcurrants
About 450 g/1 lb granulated sugar

Press the redcurrants through muslin to extract the juice; the juice must be pure. Weigh the juice and weigh out the same amount of sugar.

Gradually pour the juice into the sugar, a few drops at a time, beating with a metal spoon, as for mayonnaise. When the sugar is well mixed with the juice, continue stirring for another 20 minutes.

Pour the mixture into prepared preserving jars, still stirring. It is easier if there are two of you to do this. Put the jars, uncovered, in a cool, dry place and leave them uncovered for 2 days. Then cover and seal them.

Preserves

Cherry Preserves

Conserves de cerises

Fruits that yield a lot of juice such as redcurrants, gooseberries, cherries, and strawberries must be packed into the preserving jars so that they completely fill them. These fruits need very little water. Fill the jars and close them with the hooked metal attachment. Use a deep preserving pan. Place a cloth in the bottom of it and half-fill the pan with water. Place the jars upright in the pan, so that the water comes up to the necks. Cover the pan and put it on medium heat until it boils slowly; cherries require 20 minutes' cooking. This is an indispensable precaution to prevent the jars from bursting. After cooking, leave the jars to cool in the water. If they have been cooked sufficiently, the covers of the jars will be sealed hermetically.

Brandied Cherries

Cerises à l'eau-de-vie

Makes 750g/ 1 ½ lb

450 g/1 lb cherries, stalks trimmed in half
125 g/4 oz granulated sugar
White brandy (marc)

Pack the cherries into preserving jars, add the sugar and fill the jars with the alcohol. Seal the jars. It is not necessary to leave them in the sun, any more than it is with other fruits. The brandied cherries will take two months to mature.

Left: Bottled summer fruits,
including Marguerite's
famous brandied cherries.

183

GENERAL INDEX

Page numbers in italics refer to photographic captions.

Ajalbert 100
American colony at Giverny 69, 91, 102
Argenteuil 16—17
Automobiles, the Monets' *17*, *31*, 68, 91

Bazille, Frédéric 16
Bellio, Georges de 68, 99
Bernheim brothers 69, 75, 100, 102
Birthday, Monet's 78
Boats, the Monets' 33, 35
   studio-boat 17, 35
Bonnard, Pierre 102
Boudin, Eugène 16
Brandied preserves, Marguerite's 46, *183*
Breakfasts at Giverny *54*, 58—59
Butler, Jim 67, 98
Butler, Lily 67, 98, *99*
Butler, Marthe Hoschedé 13, 29, 41, *46*,
   75, *79*, 98
Butler, Suzanne Hoschedé 29, 35, *46*, 67,
   68, 75
Butler, Theodore *13*, *31*, 60, 68, 75, *79*, 98,
   102

Café Anglais 100
Café de Paris 76, 100, 109
Café Riche 99
Caillebotte, Gustave 34, 67, 99, 101, 102
Camondo, Isaac de 102
Carriere, Eugène 100, 102
Cassatt, Mary 102
Ceps *68*, 75, 91
Cézanne, Paul 16, 20, 54, 76, 104
Champagne *18*, 60, 89, *89*, *105*
Chanterelles *68*
Charpentier, Georges 28—29, 91, 103
Château de Rottenbourg 23, 28, 29
Chestnuts 75, *95*
Christmas lunch 78—79, *78*, *79*, *89*
Clemenceau, Georges 99, 100, 102, 104,
   105
Compotes, Marguerite's *46*, 75
Cookery notebooks, Monet's 15—16, 20,
   75—76, *124*, *134*, *150*, *162*
Coquelin 98, 100
Côte de Gaillon Racetrack picnic 17, *17*,
   79, 91
Courbet, Gustave 16
Cuisine, French, turn-of-the-century
   20—21
Curtis, Mrs. Sargent 95

Degas, Edgar 17, 102, 104
Delphine 53, 54, 105
Descaves, Lucien 100
Dinners
   at Giverny 74—75
   in Paris restaurants 98, 99—100
Doncieux, Camille *see* Monet, Camille
   Doncieux
Drouant's (restaurant) 76, 99, 100
Duncan, Isadora 104
Duran, Carolus 28
Durand-Ruel, Paul 23, 35, 60, 75, 100, 102
Dutch food, Monet's taste for 16, *54*, 58

English food, Monet's taste for 16, *54*, 58

Farman, Henry 103
Farmyards, at Giverny 42—43
Félix 42
Fishing trips 44, 67—68
Florimond 42, 44, 46, 47
Foie gras pâté, truffled *78*, *79*
Foyot (restaurant) 76
France, Anatole 102

Game, Monet's preferences 91
   carving 59—60
   pigeons 43
   rabbit and hare 43
   woodcock 78, 91, *147*
Garnishes 76
Geffroy, Gustave 99, 102
Giverny: flower-garden *18*, *21*, *23*, 33—34,
   43, 44, *46*, 68, *79*, 100—101, *101*
Giverny: house 15, 34
   colour scheme 35, 39
   dining room 35, 59, *60*, 76, 78, *91*
   entrance hall *33*, 35
   exterior *33*, 35, *44*, 60, *79*
   Japanese influence 103—104
   kitchen *15*, 35, *35*, 39, *44*, 74, *76*
   mauve drawing room 35, *79*, 91, 94, 95
   Monet's alterations to 34, 35
   paintings, Monet's private collection 102
   studio 35
   studio drawing-room 60, 68, *79*
Giverny: kitchen-garden 41, 44—47
Giverny, life at 20, 67
   annual rituals 69
   arrival 33
   daily routine 41—42, 53—60, 91

meals *see* Meals at Giverny
picnics *see* Picnics
visitors 69, 76, 90, 91, 100—104
Giverny: village 34, 69, 91
Giverny: water-garden *23*, 68, *79*, *99*, *105*
Goncourt, Edmond de 100, 103
Guitry, Lucien 76, 98, 102
Guitry, Sacha 76, 101, 103

Haundorf, Fernand 90
Helleu, Paul 101, 102, 104
Homeopathic prescription, Alice's 94
Hoschedé, Alice *see* Monet, Alice
   Hoschedé
Hoschedé, Blanche 23, 29, 41, 43, *46*, 58,
   60, 102, 103, 105
Hoschedé, Ernest 23, 28, 29, 33, 94, 100
Hoschedé, Germaine *see* Salerou,
   Germaine Hoschedé
Hoschedé, Jacques 29, 68
Hoschedé, Jean-Pierre 29, 44, 68, 78
Hoschedé, Marthe *see* Butler, Marthe
   Hoschedé
Hoschedé, Suzanne *see* Butler, Suzanne
   Hoschedé
Hotel Baudy 68, 69, 91
Hunter, Mary 95, 103
Hunting 78, 90
   picnics following 67, 69, *69*, 90—91

Ile aux Orties (Nettle Island) 35, 42
Impressionists' first exhibition 17, 23
Inventions, Michel's and Jean-Pierre's 42,
   68

Japanese bridge *99*, *105*
Japanese influence 103—104
Jongkind, Johann Barthold 16
Jourdain, Frantz 100
Joyant, Maurice 100, 102
Julien's (restaurant) 76, 100

Kitchen-garden 41, 44—47
Kuroki family 103, 105

Le Havre 16
Ledoyen (restaurant) 99
London, Monet's visits to 95

Luncheons, celebratory
  Christmas 78–79, *78*, *79*, *89*
  Monet's birthday 78
  wedding of Germaine and Albert
    Salerou *51*
  wedding of Marthe and Theodore Butler
    13
  wedding of Suzanne and Theodore
    Butler 68
Lunches at Giverny 54, 59, *60*
Lysès, Charlotte 76, 103

Maison Bleue *see* Giverny: kitchen-garden
Maison du Pressoir *see* Giverny: house
Mallarmé, Stéphane 76, 94, 95, 99, 102
Marguerite 42, 59, 74–76, 91, 102, 105
Marguéry's (restaurant) 76, 100
Mascaret picnic 79
Matisse, Henri 102
Maupassant, Guy de 75
Meals at Giverny 74
  breakfast *54*, 58–9
  dinner 74–75
  for guests 76, *91*
  lunch 54, 59, *60*
  teas 97, 102
  see also Luncheons, celebratory *and*
    Picnics
Meat, carving, Monet's custom 59
Medicinal remedies 94
Millet, Jean 20, 76
Mirbeau, Octave 34, 67, 98, 101, 102
Monet, Alice Hoschedé 28, 33
  bankruptcy and separation from Ernest
    29, 33
  daily routine at Giverny 53–54, 60
  life at Château de Rottenbourg 23, 28
  life at Giverny 20, 67, 90, 97
  life at Vétheuil 18, 29
  move to Giverny 33
Monet, Camille Doncieux 16, 18, 29, 33,
  54
Monet, Claude *1*, *21*, *31*, *46*, *54*, *58*, *192*
  childhood in Le Havre 16
  daily routine at Giverny 54–60
  early work 16
  first visit to Château de Rottenbourg 23,
    28–9
  Impressionists' first exhibition (1874) 17
  life at Argenteuil 16–17
  life at Giverny 20, 67, 97, 104–5
  life at Vétheuil 18, 29
  marriage to Camille Doncieux 16
  military service in Algeria 16
  Monet-Rodin exhibition (1889) 68
  travels 16, 95

Monet, Claude, works by
  The Basket of Grapes 42
  The Cakes 97
  decorations for Château de Rottenbourg
    29
  Hunting Trophies 74
  Impression: Sunrise 23
  Lady with a Parasol 35
  The Luncheon (1868) *54*
  Luncheon (1873) *72*
  Luncheon on the Grass 15, *73*
  Still Life with Melon 41
  Women in the Garden 69
Monet, Jean 16, 33, *54*
Monet, Michel 18, 33, 44, 68
Montgeron 23
  see also Château de Rottenbourg
Morisot, Berthe 17, 23, 102
Mushrooms, wild 68, 75, 90, 91, *116*

Namara, Marguerite 104
Natanson, Thadée 75
Nettle Island (Ile aux Orties) 35, 42
Notebooks, cookery, Monet's 15–16, 20,
  75–76, *124*, *134*, *150*, *162*

Opéra-Comique 95
Orangerie, The, Water-lily Decorations
  for *58*

Paris, trips to 95, 97, 98–100
Paris-Madrid Road Race picnic 79, 91
Paul 42, 43, 59, 60, 78, 102
Perry, Lilla Cabot 102
Perry family 90, 103
Picnics 67, 68
  Côte de Gaillon Racetrack *17*, 79
  hunting 67, *69*, 69, 90–91
  Mascaret 79
  Paris-Madrid Road Race 79, 91
Pike, Monet's preferences *44*, 75, 78, *157*
Pissarro, Camille 16, 17, 60, 102
Pissarro, Lucien 90
Potter-Palmers 95
Poultry, Monet's preferences 42, 43, *131*
  carving 59–60
Preserves, brandied, Marguerite's 46, *183*
Proust, Antonin 99
Prunier's (restaurant) 100

Raingo, Germaine 90
Raingo family 23
Renoir, Auguste 16, 17, 99, 102

Restaurants patronised by Monet 76, 98,
  99–100
Robinson, Theodore 102
Rodin, Auguste 68, 98, 100, 102, 104
Rottenbourg, Château de 23, 28, 29

Salad, Monet's preferences 60, *60*
Salerou, Albert 51
Salerou, Germaine Hoschedé 29, 42, 46,
  51, 67, 68
Salerou, Nitou 67
Salerou, Sisi *42*, 67
Sargent, John Singer 95, 102
Sisley, Alfred 16, 17, 102
Sisley, Jean and Pierre 90
Studio-boat 17, 35
Studios, Monet's, at Giverny
  first 35
  second 43, 67, 94
  third (large or Waterlily Studio) *58*, 67,
    103
Sylvain 42, 44, 54, 60, 68, 75, 91

Table settings *15*, *53*, *54*, *60*, 76
  blue Creil earthenware *53*, 76, 103
  Christmas 79, *79*, *89*
  picnic *69*
  white and yellow porcelain 76, *91*, 103
Tatin sisters 20, 76, 91
Teas at Giverny 97, 102
Theatre, visits to 98
Toulgouat, Jean-Marie 67, 68
Toussaint, Abbé 42, 68, 101
Truffaut, Georges *101*

Valéry, Paul 102
Vegetables, Monet's preferences 47, 59, 75
Vernon, town of 54, 97–98
Vétheuil 18, 29, 33
Visitors to Giverny 90, 100–104
  American 69, 91, 101, 102
  Japanese 103–104
  lunches for 76, *91*
Vuillard, Edouard 102

Water-lilies *23*, *39*
Water-lily Decorations *58*
Wedding luncheons *see* Luncheons,
  celebratory
Whistler, James McNeill 75, 76, 102, 103
Wine, Monet's preferences 60
Woodcock 78, 91, *147*
Woodcuts, Japanese, Monet's collection of
  59, 78, 103

RECIPES INDEX

Page numbers in italics refer to photographic captions.

Almond biscuits 181
Apple fritters 170
Apple meringue 175
Apple tart, upside down 166
    general 20, 46, 76
Apples, baked 172
Apples, flamed 175
Apples, fried 173
Apples with pistachios 174-175
Apricot charlotte 172
Apricot soufflé 172
Artichoke hearts, stuffed 128-129
Aspic, calves' liver in 145
Aspic, chicken in 133
Aubergine and tomato casserole 129
Aubergines, stuffed 127
Aubergines farcies 127
Aubergines aux tomates 129

Baked apples 172
Baked bananas 174
Baked beans Provençal-style 128
Baked calves' liver 143
Baked field mushrooms 126
Baked peaches *76*, 166
Baked red kidney beans 123
Banana ice cream 176, *176*
    general 59, 79
Bananas, baked 174
Bananas in red wine 175
Bananes au gratin 174
Barbue à la Dugléré 155
    general 76
Baudroie à l'americaine 156
    general 79
Beans, baked, Provençal-style 128
Beans, baked red kidney 123
Béarnaise sauce 118
Bécasse à la casserole 147
Bécasse rotie 149
Béchamel sauce 160
Beef, pickled 142
Beef à la mode, cold 137, *137*
    Marthe Butler's version 137
Beef pie 137
Beef rib with olives 145
Beignets de pommes 170
Beignets soufflés 167
Biscuit roulé 172
Biscuit de Savoie 173
Biscuits, almond 181
Biscuits, chestnut 179, *179*
    general 102

Biscuits, honey 180
Boeuf berrichon 142
Boeuf mode (Marthe Butler) 137, *137*
Bouillabaisse de morue (Cézanne) 162, *162*
    general 20, 76
Bouillon gras, pour faire un 113
Boulettes de veau 145
Braised chicken in red wine 133
Braised pigeons 148
Brandied cherries 183, *183*
Bread, cherry 174
Bread rolls, Millet's 180
    general 20, 76
Brill Dugléré-style 155
    general 76
Brioche with greengages 173
Brioches aux reines-claudes 173
Brochet au beurre blanc 44, *119*, 157, *157*
Burnt cream 174

Cabbage soup with cheese 113
Cakes
    Chestnut cake 169
    Chocolate cobblestone cake 168
    Chocolate gâteau 168
    Flat cake 170
    Genoa cake 179, *179*
    Genoese sponge 169
    Green cake 165, *165*
    Mélanie's puff pastry cheesecake 167
    Orange cake 180
    Pound cake 167
    Rich fruit cake 179, *179*
    Savoy sponge cake 173
Calves' liver, baked 143
Calves' liver in aspic 145
Canard aux navets 147
Canard à la rouennaise 149
Capon, stuffed 131
    general 79
Caroline's pancakes 181
Carottes fermières 127
Carrots, glazed 126
Cassoulet de Guitry (Lucien) 140–141
    general 76
Cèpes à la bordelaise 128
Ceps, (Monet's) recipe for 124
    general 75
Ceps Bordeaux-style 128
Cerises à l'eau-de-vie 183
Cézanne's salt cod soup 162, *162*
    general 20, 76

Chanterelles, scrambled eggs with *115*, 116, *116*
Chanterelles, Stéphane Mallarmé's recipe for 124
    general 76
Chapon farci 131
    general 79
Charlotte, apricot 172
Charlotte aux abricots 172
Charlotte Lysès's stuffed white onions 123, *123*
    general 76
Cheesecake, Mélanie's puff pastry 167
Cherries, brandied 183, *183*
Cherry bake 171
Cherry bread 174
Cherry preserves 183
Chestnut biscuits 179, *179*
    general 102
Chestnut cake 169
Chestnut soufflé 171
Chevreuil aux cynorhodons 150, *150*
Chicken, braised, in red wine 133
Chicken, fried 132
Chicken, grilled 131
Chicken in aspic 133
Chicken casserole 132
Chicken chasseur 132
Chicken with chervil 134
Chicken with crayfish butter 134, *134*
    general 100
Chicken in white wine sauce 131
Chocolate cobblestone cake 168
Chocolate cream, rich 174
Chocolate creams 175
Chocolate gâteau 168
Christmas pudding (a good one) 166
    general 79
Cinnamon toast 180
    general 102
Clafouti 171
Clear stock 112
Cold beef à la mode 137, *137*
    Martha Butler's version 137
Confiture de prunes 182
Conserver les grappes de raisins, pour 176
Conserves de cerises 183, *183*
Consommé, pour faire un bon 112
Coq au vin 133
Costriade 161
Côte de boeuf aux olives 145
Cotelettes de veau à la milanaise 144
Court-bouillon 154, 157, 160
Crabs, how to cook 157

Crayfish butter, chicken with 134, *134*
   general 100
Cream to accompany rice pudding 170
Cream of sorrel soup 111
Cream of turnip soup 112
Creams
   Burnt cream 174
   Chocolate creams 175
   Cream to accompany rice pudding 170
   Fried custard creams 171
   Mocha cream 168
   Rich chocolate cream 174
   Upside down cream 170
   Vanilla cream 169
Crème pour accompagner le pudding au riz
   170
Crème brûlée 174
Crème au chocolat 175
Crème frite 171
Crème moka 168
Crème renversée 170
Crème somptueuse 174
Crème à la vanille 169
Crêpes (Caroline) 181
Croquettes de morue 160
Croûtes aux pêches 76,166
Cuisson des crevettes et des crabes 157
Custard, savoury egg, with tomato sauce
   115
Custard creams, fried 171

Daube de bananes 175
Duck in claret sauce 149
Duck pie 150
Duck with turnips 147

Eau de sel pour la cuisson des poissons 157
Eggs
   Eggs Orsini 116
   Poached eggs au gratin 115
   Savoury egg custard with tomato sauce
     115
   Scrambled eggs *115*, 116, *116*
   Stuffed eggs 116
Eggs Orsini 116
Entrecôte bordelaise 144
Entrecôte à la briarde 140
Entrecôte marchand de vin 142
Epaule de mouton farcie 140
Escalopes Foyot 141
   general 76
Escalopes de veau à la viennoise 144

Filets de maquereaux à la flamande 156

Filets de sole à la florentine 161
   general 76
Filets de sole à la Horly 153
Filets de sole à la Véron 162
Fish
   Brill Dugléré-style 155
   Cézanne's salt cod soup 162
   Fish creole 161
   Fish soup 154
   Florentine fillets of sole 161
   Mackerel fillets in maître d'hotel sauce
     156
   Marinated fried sole 153
   Mixed fish stew 161
   Monkfish American-style 156
   Pike in white butter sauce 157
   Salt cod croquettes 160
   Sole fillets in Véron sauce 162
   Sole in shellfish sauce 154
   see also Shellfish
Fish creole 161
Fish soup 154
Flamed apples 175
Flat cake 170
Florentine fillets of sole 161
   general 76
Foie de veau en aspic 145
Foie de veau à la moissoneuse 143
Fonds d'artichauts farcis 128–129
Fresh tomato sauce 115, 119
Fried apples 173
Fried chicken 132
Fried custard creams 171
Fried woodcock 147
Fritters, apple 170
Fritters, Mélanie's soufflé 167

Galette 170
Galette feuilletée (Mélanie) 167
Galettes aux marrons 179, *179*
   general 102
Garbure 113
Garlic soup *111*, 113
Gâteau, chocolate 168
Gâteau au chocolat 168
Gâteau de marrons 169
Gâteau à l'orange 180
Gâteaux nantais 181
Gelée de groseille à froid 182
Genoa cake 179, *179*
Genoese sponge 169
Génoise 169
Gigot de chevreuil mariné 147
Glace à la banane, le 176, *176*
   general 59, 79
Glazed carrots 127

Grapes, to make raisins from 176
Grapes, to preserve whole bunches of 176
Gratin de champignons 126
Green cake 165, *165*
   general 78
Greengages, brioche with 173
Grilled chicken 131
Grilled steak with bone-marrow sauce 144
Grilled steak with mustard 140
Grilled steak with red wine sauce 142

Hard sauce 166
Haricots rouges à l'étuvée 123
Haricots secs à la provençale 128
Herb soup 112
Hollandaise sauce 118
Homard à l'americaine 155
   general 76
Homard à la Douglas 160
Homard à la Newburg 156
   general
Honey biscuits 180
Horseradish sauce 119
Huitres aux saucisses 155

Ice cream, banana 176, *176*
   general 59, 79

Jam, plum 182
Jelly, uncooked redcurrant 182

Lamb, stuffed shoulder of 140
Lamb stew, Lucien Guitry's 140–141
   general 76
Langue de boeuf au gratin 141
Leek and potato soup 111
Liver, calves', in aspic 145
Liver, calves', baked 143
Lobster American-style 155
   general 76
Lobster Douglas 160
Lobster Newburg 156
   general 75
Lucien Guitry's lamb stew 140–141
   general 76

Mackerel fillets in maître d'hotel sauce 156

Madeleines 181
Madeleines au citron 181
Maître d'hotel sauce 156
Marguéry's oxtail stew 142
    general 76
Marinated fried sole 153
Marinated haunch of venison 147
Marthe Butler's cold beef à la mode 137,
    137
Mayonnaise 119
Mélanie's puff pastry cheesecake 167
Mélanie's soufflé fritters 167
Millet's bread rolls 180
    general 20, 76
Mixed fish stew 161
Mixed vegetable soup 111
Mocha cream 168
Monkfish American-style 156
    general 79
Morels 131
    stuffed capon 131
Moules au vert 153
Mousse, strawberry 168
Mousse aux fraises 168
Mushroom purée 129
Mushrooms, baked field 126
Mussels with fresh herbs 153

Oeufs berrichons 116
Oeufs brouillés *115*, 116, *116*
    general 79
Oeufs Orsini 116
Oeufs pochés à la lyonnaise 115
Oeufs renversés à la tomate 115
Oignons blancs farcis (Charlotte Lysès) 23,
    123
    general 76
Omelette, soufflé 171
Omelette soufflée 171
Onions, white, stuffed (Charlotte Lysès's)
    123, *123*
Orange cake 180
Ox tongue au gratin 141
Oxtail stew, Marguéry's 142
    general 76
Oyster soup 153
Oysters with sausages 155

Pain de cerises 174
Pain de Gênes 179, *179*
Pain perdu 181
Palets au miel 180
Palette de porc Sacha (Guitry) 140, *162*
    general 76
Pancakes, Caroline's 181

Partridge with cabbage 149
Pâté, rabbit 148-149
Pâté de boeuf 137
Pâté de canard 150
Pâté de pommes de terre 126−127
Pavé au chocolat 168
Peaches, baked *76*, 166
Peaches, stewed 173
Pêches à la Bourdaloue 173
Perdrix aux choux 149
Petits pains (Millet) 180
    general 20, 76
Pets-de-nonne 167
Pickled beef 142
Pigeon stew 148
    general 75
Pigeons, braised 148
Pigeons en compote 148
    general 75
Pigeons forestière 148
Pike in white butter sauce *44*, *119*, 157,
    157
Pistachios, apples with 174−175
Plum jam 182
Poached eggs au gratin 115
Poached truffles 124
Poisson à la créole 161
Pommes au beurre 172
Pommes flambées 175
Pommes frites 173
Pommes meringuées 175
Pommes aux pistaches 174−175
Poor knights 181
Pork, shoulder of, Sacha Guitry's 140
    general 76
Pork chops Foyot 141
    general 76
Potage à la Dauphine 112
Potage fontange 111
Potage Germiny 111
Potato pie 126−127
Potato soup, leek and 111
Potine de lapin 148−149
Poulet au beurre d'écrevisses 134, *134*
    general 100
Poulet au certfeuil 134
Poulet chasseur 132
Poulet en cocotte 132
Poulet frit 132
Poulet en gelée 133
Poulet grillé 131
Poulet à la périgourdine 131
Pound cake 167
Prawns, how to cook 157
Preserves, cherry 183
Pudding, Christmas 166
Puff pastry cheesecake, Mélanie's 167
Purée de champignons 129

Quatre-quarts 167
Queue de boeuf en hochepot (Marguéry)
    142
    general 76

Rabbit pâté 148-149
Raisins, to make from grapes 176
Recette pour les cèpes, ma 124
    general 76
Recette de girolles (Mallarmé) 124, *124*
    general 76
Redcurrant jelly 182
Rich chocolate cream 174
Rich fruit cake 179, *179*
Rich stock 113
Roast woodcock 149
Rolls, bread, Millet's 180
    general 20, 76

Sacha Guitry's shoulder of pork 140, *162*
    general 76
Salt cod croquettes 160
Salt cod soup, Cézanne's 162, *162*
    general 20, 76
Salt water fish stock 157
Sauce béarnaise 118
Sauce hollandaise 118
Sauce mayonnaise 119
Sauce pour le pudding 166
Sauce raifort, dite Radimsky 119
Sauce tartar 118
Sauce tomate 119
Sauce à la tomate 118
Sauces
    Béchamel sauce 160
    Béarnaise sauce 118
    Fresh tomato sauce 115, 119
    Hard sauce 166
    Hollandaise sauce 118
    Horseradish sauce 119
    Maître d'hotel sauce 156
    Mayonnaise 119
    Tartar sauce 118
    Tomato sauce 118
    Véron sauce 162
    White butter sauce *119*, 157
Sausages, oysters with 155
Savoury egg custard with tomato sauce
    115
Savoy sponge cake 173
Scones 179, *179*
    general 102
Scrambled eggs *115*, 116, *116*
    general 79

Sêcher les raisins, pour 176
Shellfish 157
    Lobster American-style 154
    Lobster Douglas 160
    Lobster Newburg 156
    Mussels with fresh herbs 153
    Oyster soup 153
    Oysters with sausages 155
Shoulder of pork, Sacha Guitry's 140, *162*
    general 76
Shrimps, how to cook 157
Sole, Florentine fillets of 161
Sole, marinated fried 153
Sole fillets in Véron sauce 162
Sole in shellfish sauce 154
    general 20
Sole à la normande 154
    general 20
Sorrel soup, cream of 111
Soufflé, apricot 172
Soufflé, chestnut 171
Soufflé à l'abricot 172
Soufflé fritters, Mélanie's 167
Soufflé aux marrons 171
Soufflé omelette 171
Soupe à l'ail 111, 113
Soupe aux herbes 112
Soupe aux poireaux et pommes de terre 111
Soupe aux poissons 154
Soups
    Cabbage soup with cheese 113
    Clear stock 112
    Cream of sorrel soup 111
    Cream of turnip soup 112
    Fish soup 154
    Garlic soup *111*, 113
    Herb soup 112
    Leek and potato soup 111
    Mixed vegetable soup 111

Oyster soup 153
    Rich stock 113
    Salt cod soup 162, *162*
Steak, grilled, with bone-marrow sauce 144
Steak, grilled, with mustard 140
Steak, grilled, with red wine sauce 142
Stéphane Mallarmé's recipe for chanterelles 124, *124*
Stewed peaches 173
Stock, clear 112
Stock, rich 113
Stock, salt water fish 157
Strawberry mousse 168
Stuffed artichoke hearts 128–129
Stuffed aubergines 127
Stuffed capon 131
    general 79
Stuffed eggs 116
Stuffed shoulder of lamb 140
Stuffed tomatoes 126
Stuffed white onions, Charlotte Lysès's 123, *123*
    general 76
Swiss roll 172

Tartar sauce 118
Tarte Tatin 166
    general 20, 46, 76
Toast, cinnamon 180
    general 102
Toasts à la canelle 180
    general 102
Tomato sauce 118
Tomato sauce, fresh 115, 119
Tomatoes, stuffed 126
Tomatoes farcies 126

Tongue, ox, au gratin 141
Truffes à la serviette 124
Truffles, poached 124
Truffles, with scrambled eggs 115, *115*, 116
Turnip soup, cream of 112

Uncooked redcurrant jelly 182
Upside down apple tart 166
    general 20, 46, 76
Upside down cream 170

Vanilla cream 169
Veal cutlets, Milanese-style 144
Veal forcemeat balls 145
Veal with olives 141
Veau aux olives 141
Vegetable soup, mixed 111
Venison, marinated haunch of 147
Venison with rosehips 150, *150*
Véron sauce 162
Vert-vert 165, *165*
    general 78
Vienna schnitzel 144

Welsh rarebit 123
    general
White butter sauce *119*, 157
Woodcock, fried 147
Woodcock, roasted 149

Yorkshire pudding 143
    general 76

PICTURE CREDITS

Claude Monet c. 1920.